A STUDY OF BEN JONSON

A STUDY OF
BEN JONSON

by

Algernon Charles Swinburne

Edited with an introduction by

HOWARD B. NORLAND

UNIVERSITY OF NEBRASKA PRESS · LINCOLN

First Bison Book printing November, 1969

*The text of the Bison Book edition is reproduced
from the 1889 edition published by Worthington Co.,
New York.*

CONTENTS

CONTENTS

INTRODUCTION

FROM the days when Robert Herrick and Richard Brome sealed themselves to the "Tribe of Ben," Ben Jonson has had loyal supporters, but in the nineteenth century admirers of the man who had overshadowed Shakespeare in his own time were scarce. It is true that Coleridge had singled out the plot of *The Alchemist* for special praise,[1] but the Romantic and Victorian periods found Jonson's neoclassical and satiric spirit alien. Poets and critics objected to Jonson's scorn and coarseness, and scholars were busily engaged in proving his malignity, particularly toward Shakespeare. The voices of William Gifford and Octavius Gilchrist who came to Jonson's defense in the early part of the century[2] for the most part went unheard. The bardolatry of the Romantics continued, as did the enthusiasm for Christopher Marlowe. In 1875 Gifford's edition of Jonson, slightly revised by Colonel Francis Cunningham, was reissued, and J. A. Symonds in 1886 offered a critique of Ben Jonson, that apparently went largely unread. Finally, a new "son of Ben" emerged in the unlikely

[1] See p. 40 of the present text and my explanatory note at the end of this volume.

[2] See p. 3 of this text and my explanatory note.

figure of Algernon Charles Swinburne. Not only did Swinburne's predilections for sentiment and sentimentality in his own verse and his preference for lyrical tragedy make him an unlikely admirer of the stolid comic playwright, but also Swinburne was associated in the public mind with the Pre-Raphaelites and the "art for art's sake" school of criticism, which diametrically opposed the didactic theory embraced by Jonson. Yet Swinburne's *Study of Ben Jonson*, published first in article form in 1888 and then as a book in 1889, probably did more than any other single work to return the satirical genius of the seventeenth century to critical prominence and ultimately to a long overdue re-evaluation. Swinburne did not overturn the critical prejudices that had been solidifying through the Victorian age—he was too bound up in the aesthetic theory of his time for that—but he did by his enthusiastic appraisal send his readers back to the comic master with a new appreciation of Jonson's art.[3]

[3] Several of the reviews of *A Study of Ben Jonson* comment on Swinburne forcing his readers to return to the work in question, but not all consider it meritorious. One who does is the anonymous reviewer in *The Dial* who writes, "It is, perhaps, the first of the many merits of Mr. Swinburne's critical studies that they inevitably send their readers to the works of the poet under consideration" (X [1890], 341–342).

Swinburne's success in revivifying the image of Ben Jonson resulted to a great extent from his conception of the function of the critic, which he believed was "first to discern what is good, and then to discover how and in what way it is so."[4] This view proved to be both his blessing and his curse as a critic: it led to charges that he wrote nothing but indiscriminate panegyric, but at the same time it stimulated reading and elevated literature to a higher plane of existence. Swinburne is one of the greatest friends literature has ever had, for by devoting much of his life to "the noble pleasure of praising,"[5] he fostered an environment of appreciation of the human spirit in an age that was becoming increasingly utilitarian. This zealous missionary of literature had little patience with negative criticism: even though he was an admirer of Coleridge's poetry, he regarded Coleridge's criticism as a "fusion of malevolence with incompetence, of prejudice with misconception, of would-be candour with obvious prepossession."[6] Regardless of

[4] "Morris's 'Life and Death of Jason,'" *The Complete Works of Algernon Charles Swinburne*, ed. Sir Edmund Gosse and Thomas J. Wise (London, 1925–27), XV, 50. Hereafter this edition of *The Complete Works* will be cited as Bonchurch, its common name, with volume and page numbers.

[5] Bonchurch XVI, 372.

[6] Bonchurch XII, 436.

this instance of scorn, Swinburne did adopt some
aspects of Coleridgean criticism, as we shall see, but
he did not imitate the method or essential conception. He turned instead to Charles Lamb, whom
he had admired from boyhood, for his approach
and his technique. Some thirty years after Lamb's
Specimens of the English Dramatic Poets had inspired him at Eton,[7] Gosse reports that Swinburne
picked up a copy of the famous anthology and
announced, " 'That book taught me more than any
other in the world,—that and the Bible.' "[8] The
"specimens" included what Lamb considered to be
the very best passages from the Renaissance playwrights along with commentary pointing out why
they are particularly noteworthy. No play is printed
in full for a total appraisal; rather the reader is
invited to share Lamb's appreciative response to
individual verses and scenes. The comments themselves usually emphasize the poetry at the expense
of the dramatic situation. Lamb's approach is not
that of a scholar or of a critic but that of a lover
singling out the features of grace and beauty which

[7] Swinburne indicates Lamb's effect on him at Eton in a
letter to A. H. Bullen (July 19, 1882), *The Swinburne Letters*,
ed. Cecil Y. Lang (New Haven, 1959–62), IV, 279–280.

[8] *The Life of Algernon Charles Swinburne*, Bonchurch
XIX, 15.

he most admires and ignoring the blemishes that mar the totality. It was Lamb who introduced Swinburne to the raptures of literature and more particularly to the drama of Shakespeare's contemporaries. The romance with the Elizabethans begun at Eton became a lifelong passion, and with it came a literary outlook that was later bolstered by theory but remained essentially unchanged. William Archer in 1893 pointed out the major liability of Lamb's and his disciple Swinburne's approach: "Their knowledge of the Elizabethan period is imperfect on the historical side, and on the literary side so intimate as to be uncritical."[9]

Swinburne does at times allow his ardor to dim his judgment, but he adopted principles that justified his outlook and shaped his response. Much of his theory came from the Romantic poets who were because of his sensibility his natural mentors. From Blake, Coleridge, and Shelley he acquired the concepts and the terminology to articulate his response, and by Victor Hugo's influence he was weaned

[9] "Webster, Lamb, and Swinburne," *The New Review*, VIII (1893), 97. George Bernard Shaw also comments that Swinburne indiscriminately "swallowed the Elizabethan dramatists" as a result of reading Lamb ("The Genius and Influence of Swinburne," by Sir Edmund Gosse *et al*, *The Bookman*, XXXVI [June 1909], 129).

away from the "art for art's sake" school of criticism to a greater social awareness of the meaning
of literature.[10] Swinburne in his eclectic manner
fused the critical principles he adopted into a body
of theory that modifies as it extends the positions
of his forebears. Unfortunately, his choice of masters did not include a practical dramatic critic, but
that was a part of the heritage of the Victorian;
and unfortunately, too, the contemporary theater
did not interest Swinburne. He flatly rejected both
the stock melodrama of his age and the new drama
developing from the impetus of Ibsen. Although
Swinburne loved the old drama to which Lamb had
introduced him and wrote tragedies himself in imitation of the Elizabethans, his dramatic sense never
developed to include the element of staging. Only
one of his own plays was ever produced in his lifetime, and the production proved that it was more
properly meant for the study,[11] like most of the

[10] For Hugo's influence on Swinburne, see Thomas E. Connolly, *Swinburne's Theory of Poetry* (Albany, N. Y., 1964), p.
4 and *passim*.

[11] *Locrine*, published in 1887, was produced at St. George's
Hall March 20, 1899, but it apparently closed after one per-
formance. See Allardyce Nicoll, *A History of Late Nineteenth
Century Drama, 1850–1900* (Cambridge, 1949), II, 589. Georges
Lafourcade reports that *Chastelard* (1865) "was very nearly
produced by Lugné-Poe in 1904, in a French version by

other plays written by English poets in the nine-teenth century. Following Shelley, Coleridge, and Lamb, Swinburne responded to plays as poetry rather than drama, and, as a result, his criticism at times suffers from prejudice and myopia.

His approach to Jonson is signalled at the be-ginning of his study by his placement of Jonson on the side of the giants as opposed to the gods. His opening sentence clarifies the division: "If poets may be divided into two exhaustive but not exclusive classes,—the gods of harmony and creation, the giants of energy and invention,—the supremacy of Shakespeare among the gods of English verse is not more unquestionable than the supremacy of Jonson among its giants" (p. 3). The distinction is essentially between the imaginative artist and the rational artisan, or to put it another way, between the celebration of the spirit and the depiction of the mundane.[12] In the Jonson camp are Dryden and Byron, whose feet are squarely planted in this world, but in the assembly of Shakespeare are Milton and Shelley, who severed their earthly bonds

---

Maeterlinck, at the Théâtre de l'Œuvre. Since then, no pro-ducer has been brave enough to attempt the task" (*Swin-burne, A Literary Biography* [London, 1932], p. 225).

[12] Connolly defines the distinction as one "between spiritual idealists and rational realists" (p. 31).

to soar into the heavens. The classification is useful, even if somewhat over-simplified, for by it Swinburne indicates his priorities as well as his measure of judgment. In placing imagination on a higher plane than reason, Swinburne is following the lead of both Blake and Shelley who rejected reason as the tool to real understanding or the means to integration with the universe. Imagination synthesizes, while reason dissects.[13] Swinburne elaborates on the meaning of his dichotomy as he emphasizes his preference for spiritual imagination in his study of George Chapman: the "substitution of an intellectual for an ideal end, of energetic mental action for passionate spiritual emotion as the means towards that end, is as good a test as may be taken of the difference in kind rather than in degree between the first and the second order of imaginative artists."[14] In the first order he places Shakespeare and Marlowe, and in the second Jonson and Chapman. On other occasions he places Webster on the side of the "gods" of imagination and Ford on the side of the "giants" of invention.[15]

Swinburne's theory of imagination owes something to Coleridge, but in *A Study of Ben Jonson*

[13] Cf. Connolly, pp. 34–35.
[14] Bonchurch XII, 242.
[15] Bonchurch XI, 281 and XII, 377.

Swinburne applies his theory negatively in order to prove why Ben Jonson is not as good as a Shakespeare. Again and again Swinburne comments on Jonson's studied realism and his analytical bent. Swinburne complains, "There is nothing accidental in the work of Ben Jonson: no casual inspiration, no fortuitous impulse," and further, "this crowning and damning defect of a tedious and intolerable realism was even exceptionally wilful and premeditated" (p. 9). Later in a more specific discussion of Jonson's poetry, Swinburne interjects, "anatomical particularity . . . too often defaces the serious verse of Jonson with grotesque if not gross deformity of detail" (p. 49). Jonson in Swinburne's view is too earthbound: he lacks the harmony of passion and "sublimity" that "is the test of imagination as distinguished from invention or from fancy."[16] The reason, as Swinburne saw it, for Jonson's failing was an over-emphasis on "the weight of matter, the solidity of meaning, the significance and purpose of the thing suggested or presented" (p. 6). This explains Jonson's lack of success in the comical satires, which Swinburne termed "magnificent mistakes" (p. 15), and an over-emphasis on meaning continued

[16] Bonchurch XI, 271.

to plague Jonson's artistic technique, though in his best works his genius proved too strong for his theory (p. 19). Swinburne sums up this aspect of Jonson by identifying him with "the too studious and industrious Martha" (p. 27).

One result of the predominance of intellect over emotion was what Swinburne termed a lack of "singing power which answers in verse to the odour of a blossom, to the colouring of a picture, to the flavour of a fruit" (p. 4). In other words, Jonson's poetry lacks that extra dimension that invokes the senses to a full response. This emphasis on the aesthetic response, no doubt, derives from the "art for art's sake" school of poetry inculcated in Swinburne by Dante Rossetti and his Pre-Raphaelite friends to whom Swinburne had earlier been attached. It was probably also as much this earlier influence as natural Victorian prudery, which Swinburne himself decried, that caused him to be repelled by what he considered Jonson's coarseness. Swinburne was by no means an enemy to sensuality, as the shocked public found when he published his *Poems and Ballads* (1866) and later his *Lesbia Brandon* (1877), but he did object to the grossness of references to the bodily processes, and he was repelled by a lack of subtlety in allusion to physical love.[17] For this reason particularly Swinburne found Jonson's epigrams repugnant and hardly worthy of comment. It was this perspective, too, that relegated *Bartholomew Fair* to a position "among the minor and coarser masterpieces of comic art" (p. 62).

What Swinburne demonstrates by his critical position is that his interest is more in the poetic than in the dramatic of Jonson's plays and further that his taste is attuned to lyrical tragedy rather than to satirical comedy. In both of these preferences he is very much a man of his time, but in addition, his personal fastidiousness and his withdrawal from the everyday world to a life of the spirit at Putney made him an even less likely interpreter of the robust and gregarious Jonson. Swinburne's lack of comic appreciation and of satiric understanding colored his response to Jonson's dramatic art, particularly in the more farcical comedies. In his discussion of *Epicoene*, for instance, Swinburne comments, "The Nemesis of the satirist is upon him [Jonson]: . . . he cannot be happy in his work

[17] Perhaps one reason for his sensitivity concerning physical love was his apparent inability to have a normal love relationship with the opposite sex. Many writers have commented on this, but see particularly Cecil Y. Lang, "Swinburne's Lost Love," *PMLA*, LXXIV (1959), 123–130.

without some undertone of sarcasm. . . . His wit is wonderful—admirable, laughable, laudable—it is not in the fullest and the deepest sense delightful. It is radically cruel, contemptuous, intolerant: . . . there is something in this great classic writer of the bull-baiting or bear-baiting brutality of his age" (p. 51). Even in the midst of lavish praise for *Volpone* and *The Alchemist*, Swinburne cannot resist adding, "Scorn and indignation are but too often the motives or the mainsprings of [Jonson's] comic art" (p. 39).

Swinburne's failure to understand Jonson's satiric method led him to judge Jonson's comedies from the same perspective that he judged Shakespeare's, but his approach is even more appropriate to tragedy than to romantic comedy. However, in this Swinburne was but following the line laid down by Coleridge. Both emphasized character over plot, and both measured characterization in terms of a nineteenth-century standard of sympathy and moral goodness. Coleridge, criticizing *Volpone*, remarks that that play is "the strongest proof" of "how impossible it is to keep up any pleasurable interest in a tale, in which there is no goodness of heart in any of the prominent characters."[18] Swin-

[18] *Coleridge's Miscellaneous Criticism*, ed. Thomas Middleton Raysor (Cambridge, Mass., 1936), p. 55.

burne did not stress the moral implications of
Jonson's characters to the extent of Coleridge; as
a matter of fact, Swinburne singles out Volpone as
the one character in Jonson's plays that is represented with more sympathy than all of his other
dramatic figures, but Swinburne makes clear that
it is an "intellectual" rather than a "moral sympathy" (p. 30). It was the preponderance of "intellect" again in Swinburne's view that prevented
Jonson from infusing humanity into his characters
or from feeling sympathetic attachment to them.
In Swinburne's words, "Love and hatred, sympathy and antipathy, are superseded and supplanted by pure scientific curiosity: the clear glow
of serious or humorous emotion is replaced by the
dry light of analytical investigation" (p. 29). Swinburne in a sense came to Jonson's comedies from
the wrong end by first evaluating the characters by
his own standards rather than by seeing them in
their dramatic context or in terms of Jonson's
satiric purpose.

However, he did arrive at an understanding and
an appreciation of Jonson's architectonic skill. Unlike his earliest mentor, Charles Lamb, who did
not come to grips with a work as a whole, but rather
after the manner of Coleridge, Swinburne was

supremely conscious of the total design. Yet it was not Coleridge's "organic unity" which is basically plot-oriented that Swinburne sought; instead he looked for the "harmony" that encompasses all the elements and qualities of a work. Harmony includes character, action, tone, thought, and everything else distinguishable in a work of literature brought into a comprehensive relationship that creates a unified effect. The modern term that is most closely synonymous with Swinburne's "harmony" is "artistic unity," but even that term fails to embrace all that Swinburne meant. Although Swinburne at times applied the term harmony to the conjunction of specific parts of the total design, his full meaning is indicated in his discussion of why Byron and Ford are not in "the higher order of poets": "in the verse of neither is there that instant and sensible melody which comes only of a secret and sovereign harmony of the whole nature, and which comes of it inevitably and unmistakably."[19] In other words, harmony involves the total being of the work and is perceived not by analysis but by an intuitive aesthetic response. Swinburne usually restricted his large concept of harmony to "the gods of creation" where the term "sublimity"

[19] Bonchurch XII, 397.

means much the same thing,[20] but for Jonson, the Enceladus of the Titans, the greatest of all "the giants of invention,"[21] the concept becomes appropriate. After first admitting a personal preference for *Volpone*, Swinburne says of *The Alchemist*: "Such perfection of plot, with such multiplicity of characters—such ingenuity of incident, with such harmony of construction—can be matched, we may surely venture to say, nowhere in the whole vast range of comic invention—nowhere in the whole wide world of dramatic fiction" (p. 54). Swinburne's aesthetic response appears to have come "inevitably and unmistakably," overpowering his private taste.

Swinburne has much more to say of Jonson's dramatic designs and praises certain aspects of the whole, but nowhere else does he come so close to making Jonson a "god." When he raises the question of the totality of the work, he most often finds the integration of the elements wanting. For instance, he comments that in *Every Man out of his Humour* "the component parts . . . fail to compose a coherent or harmonious work of art" (p. 16), and he declares the problem of *The Devil is an Ass* to be the lack of connection between parts and the

[20] See, for example, Swinburne's discussion of the "sublimity" of *Doctor Faustus* (Bonchurch XI, 273–274).

[21] See p. 3 of this text and my explanatory note.

incongruity of "serious sentiment and noble emotion" in the satire (pp. 65–66). Swinburne further
criticizes the mixture of "human interest" with
"allegorical satire" in *The Devil is an Ass* (p. 67),
but interestingly in *The Staple of News*, he discovers "fusion without confusion" as the dramatic
allegory of the prodigal and the satire of the News
Exchange become one, and he rates what Dryden
had called one of the "dotages"[22] "third" or
"fourth" among Jonson's works (pp. 74–75). Swinburne's aesthetic response appears this time to have
played him false, for even if we accept a unified
design, which most modern critics do not, we must
find it difficult to understand Swinburne's enthusiasm on aesthetic grounds.

What apparently attracted Swinburne to *The
Staple of News* was what he regarded as an acute
observation of men and manners, for he sees in the
work a particular relevance to the journalism of his
own day as he comments on the prophetic nature
of the satire. In other words, Swinburne appreci-
ates Jonson's social consciousness which in this
instance has a universality of appeal that in Swinburne's view much of Jonson's work lacks. Para-
doxically the very topicality of Jonson's satire

---

[22] See p. 80 of this text and my explanatory note.

becomes universal for Swinburne because of his unpleasant personal experience with unscrupulous newsmongers of his own day.[23] It is apparently this concern for social consciousness, inculcated in Swinburne by his idol, Victor Hugo, that also led Swinburne to devote nearly a third of his book to the *Discoveries*. Not only does he regard "a single leaf" of Jonson's *Discoveries* to be "worth all his lyrics, tragedies, elegies, and epigrams together" (p. 124), but also he considers "Jonson's notes or observations on men and morals, on principles and on facts . . . superior to Bacon's in truth of insight, in breadth of view, in vigour of reflection and in concision of eloquence" (p. 129). What particularly appeals to Swinburne is the ethical comment on human character which reveals universal moral truth, but what he failed to realize

[23] Because of Swinburne's unusual appearance and eccentric habits, he became the object of caricature and willful misunderstanding by contemporary journalists. Particularly after the publication of the *Poems and Ballads* in 1866, Swinburne was subjected to slurs on his character by the scandal-hunting members of the daily press as well as to lampoons and direct attacks in magazines. See particularly Robert Buchanan's unsigned review of *Poems and Ballads* in the *Atheneum* (1866), his "The Session of the Poets" in the *Spectator* (1866), and his "The Fleshly School of Poetry," published under the pseudonym "Thomas Maitland," in the *Contemporary Review* (1871).

was that this work is essentially a commonplace book of quotations and paraphrases gathered from Jonson's extensive reading, gathered apparently for the same reasons that excited Swinburne's admiration. In this perspective the spirit of Jonson and the spirit of Swinburne are one.

Only in this one area do these two diverse poets find a common ground; only here can Swinburne be truly sealed to the "Tribe of Ben." And like the "sons" of the seventeenth century, Swinburne indulges in unqualified panegyric that shows his critical method in its baldest form. In the manner of his first and most influential mentor, Charles Lamb, Swinburne presents "specimens" and then points out the features that are particularly worthy of praise. However, even in the earlier critical discussion of the plays and poems, Swinburne is generous in his appreciation of the art forms and mental outlook so alien to his own temperament and aesthetic theory. I have concentrated on the differences between Swinburne and Jonson in critical perspective in order to show why Swinburne responded to Jonson as he did, but Swinburne himself almost never failed to find something to praise in every work of Jonson, even those he most disliked. The ultimate effect is positive and the service to Jonson immeasureable, for by it the reader is stimulated to return to Jonson's works for a re-appraisal. Sir Edmund Gosse in evaluating Swinburne's work after his death in 1909 commented, "Swinburne's most active influence on living literature is in the direction of criticism. This sounds paradoxical, since he was not a very safe critic. But he introduced, he actually invented, an attitude, or approach to literature which has affected every one who tries to write about poetry with any distinction. The temperature of his praise, the fulness of note in his generous appreciation, were higher and louder than had ever been met with in print before his day."[24] Swinburne's enthusiasm for literature, even that which conflicts with his own artistic sentiments, is indeed contagious. He may from our point of view appear at times narrow-minded, but he is always magnanimous and never dull.

The Text

A Study of Ben Jonson was first published as four articles in two periodicals: Part I in *The Nineteenth Century*, XXIII (1888), 603–616 (April),

[24] "The Genius and Influence of Swinburne," *The Bookman*, XXXVI (June 1909), 127.

which included pp. 3–34 of the present text, and
693–715 (May), which printed pp. 35–89 of this
text; and Parts II and III in *The Fortnightly Review*, L(o.s.)(1888), 24–38 (July) and 425–447 (October), respectively. In 1889, the text for the book
was composed by Spottiswoode and Company, New
Street Square, London, apparently from a corrected
and slightly revised copy of the articles, for the
format and editorial practices in the two articles
printed in *The Nineteenth Century* were adopted
by the printer of the book, except that marginal
headings were added; the different editorial practices of *The Fortnightly Review* were apparently
adjusted in the parts first appearing in that periodical in order to coincide with the practices adopted
in the first part of the book. A collation of the
periodical publication against the text of the book
revealed several variations, consisting for the most
part in punctuation differences, some of which are
obvious corrections, though others appear to result
from authorial revision, and still others may result
from compositorial errors. More important, fifteen
substantive changes were observed; of these one is
obviously a correction (change from "by" to "to,"
p. 73, l. 5), one a new error (change from "belief"
to "relief" in a quotation from *Discoveries*, p. 176,

1. 19), and one is the omission of three paragraphs from *The Fortnightly Review* (between lines 10 and 11 on p. 113), which were probably blue-pencilled by the author; but the remaining twelve substantive changes clearly suggest authorial revision.

The book was published in 1889 by Chatto and Windus in London and by the Worthington Company in New York. The printer of the London publication is identified on the verso of the half-title page as Spottiswoode and Company, London; and the Press of J. J. Little and Company, Astor Place, New York, is named on the verso of the title page as the printer of the New York publication. The pagination of the New York and London printings is identical except that the New York printing lacks a half-title page and, following the fly-title page, a leaf which is blank on the recto and contains an advertisement of Swinburne's books published by Chatto and Windus on the verso. In addition, the London printing includes a final leaf with a blank verso and with the publisher's colophon on the recto, as well as a thirty-two page advertisement of books published by Chatto and Windus.[25] A machine collation of one copy each

[25] A full bibliographical description of the London text, which also exactly fits the New York text except for the

of the London and New York publications[26] reveals that different title-pages were prepared, but the remainder of the text in both copies originates from the same plates. However, in three instances (p. 23, ll. 10–11; p. 49, ll. 3–4; and p. 148, ll. 9–10) line settings vary in the two copies. In addition, a difference in the distribution of lines per page occurs on five successive pages: the New York copy prints an additional line at the bottom of p. 85, and from that point on to the end of Part I on p. 89, the last line of type on each page in the American copy is the first line of type on the following page in the English copy. This difference in the distribution of lines of type per page would suggest that the London copy represents a correction in the lineation of the New York copy; this would seem to support the practice described by Flora V. Livingston of publishing Swinburne's "American editions" from advance sheets.[27] How-

differences just described, can be found in Thomas J. Wise, *A Bibliography of the Writings in Prose and Verse of Algernon Charles Swinburne*, Bonchurch XX, 237–238.

[26] The London copy used is the one owned by the Newberry Library in Chicago, and the New York copy used is the one owned by the Gene Eppley Library at the University of Nebraska at Omaha.

[27] *Swinburne's Proof Sheets and American First Editions* (Cambridge, Mass., 1920), p. 31.

ever, the identification of an American press would
indicate that for the American publication the
sheets were printed in America, and because
eighteen errors appearing in the English copy are
corrected in the American copy and only two new
errors are evident, the New York printing must
derive from the corrected plates used for the London printing. The two new errors that occur in
the American copy can be explained by damage
to the plates, for both appear on the margins: on
p. 150, l. 9, a comma is omitted on the right
margin, and on p. 176, l. 7, the single quotation
mark has apparently slipped and has been replaced
in reverse order, which makes it appear to be a
comma. Investigation of evidence of broken or
damaged type further supports that the American copy was printed after the English copy,
for of seventeen clear instances of broken or damaged type appearing only in the London printing,
thirteen are in the running heads, ten of which are
damage to the capital "J," which was apparently
particularly fragile. These characters were evidently replaced before the American printing, but
the American copy contains many more instances
of broken type that do not appear in the London
copy.

Apparently then Spottiswoode and Company in London set the type for the book from a corrected and slightly revised copy of the articles first published in *The Nineteenth Century* and *The Fortnightly Review*. The sheets for Chatto and Windus were run off, and then corrected plates were shipped to New York, where the Press of J. J. Little and Company printed the American copies for the Worthington Company. Even though the American printing has the disadvantage of containing more instances of broken type, because of its greater accuracy it has been reproduced as the text of this edition. Printing variations between the present text and the London copy as well as substantive, punctuation, and spelling variations between the present text and the periodical publication of the work are recorded in the textual notes immediately following the text.

Explanatory notes identifying the allusions and references in Swinburne's critical discussion are to be found at the end of this volume.

I wish to thank the Gene Eppley Library at the University of Nebraska at Omaha for permission to reproduce their copy of the New York printing of Swinburne's *Study of Ben Jonson* for this edition. Thanks are also due to the Newberry Library and the Northwestern-Newberry Melville Edition Project for allowing me to use their Hinman Collator to collate the New York and London copies of the text. To my colleagues who assisted me in tracking down the many allusions that fill the pages of Swinburne's criticism I owe a deep debt of gratitude. In addition, Professor Stanley Vandersall of the Classics Department at the University of Nebraska kindly aided me in the translation of the Latin and Greek quotations. My friend and colleague, Professor Robert Knoll, is responsible for the impetus to embark on this project. I alone am responsible for its failings.

HOWARD B. NORLAND

University of Nebraska
Lincoln

I. COMEDIES, TRAGEDIES,
AND MASQUES

I

COMEDIES, TRAGEDIES, AND MASQUES

IF poets may be divided into two exhaustive but not exclusive classes,—the gods of harmony and creation, the giants of energy and invention,—the supremacy of Shakespeare among the gods of English verse is not more unquestionable than the supremacy of Jonson among its giants. Shakespeare himself stands no higher above Milton and Shelley than Jonson above Dryden and Byron. Beside the towering figure of this Enceladus the stature of Dryden seems but that of an ordinary man, the stature of Byron—who indeed can only be classed among giants by a somewhat licentious or audacious use of metaphor—seems little higher than a dwarf's. Not even the ardour of his most fanatical worshippers, from the date of Cartwright and Randolph to the date of Gilchrist and Gifford, could exaggerate the actual greatness of his various and marvellous energies. No giant ever came so near to the ranks of the gods : were it possible for one not born a god to become divine by dint of ambition and devotion, this glory would have crowned the Titanic labours of Ben Jonson.   There is something heroic and magnificent in his lifelong dedication of all his gifts and all his powers to the service of the art he had elected as the business of all his life and the aim of all his aspiration.   And the result also was magnificent : the flowers of his growing have every quality but one which belongs to the rarest and finest among flowers : they have colour, form, variety, fertility, vigour : the one thing they want is fragrance.   Once or twice only in all his indefatigable career of toil and triumph did he achieve what was easily and habitually accomplished by men otherwise unworthy to be named in the same day with him ; by men who would have avowed themselves unworthy to un-loose the latchets of his shoes.   That singing power which answers in verse to the odour of a blossom, to the colouring of a picture, to the flavour of a fruit,—that quality without which they may be good, commendable, admirable, but cannot be delightful,—was not, it should seem, a natural gift of this great writer's : hardly now and then could his industry attain to it by some exceptional touch

of inspiration or of luck. It is 'above all strange-
ness' that a man labouring under this habitual dis-
qualification should have been competent to recognize with accurate and delicate discernment an
occasion on which he had for once risen above his
usual capacity—a shot by which he had actually
hit the white: but the lyrical verses which Ben
Jonson quoted to Drummond as his best have
exactly the quality which lyrical verse ought to
have and which their author's lyrical verse almost
invariably misses; the note of apparently spontaneous, inevitable, irrepressible and impeccable
music. They might have been written by Coleridge or Shelley. But Ben, as a rule,—a rule
which is proved by the exception—was one of the
singers who could not sing; though, like Dryden,
he could intone most admirably; which is more—
and much more—than can truthfully be said for
Byron. He, however, as well as Dryden, has one
example of lyrical success to show for himself,
as exceptional and as unmistakable as Jonson's.
The incantation in *Œdipus*, brief as it is, and the
first four stanzas of the incantation in *Manfred*,
imitative as they are, reveal a momentary sense of
music, a momentary command of the instrument
employed, no less singular and no less absolute.

But Jonson, at all points the greatest and most genuine poet of the three, has achieved such a success more than once; has nearly achieved it, or has achieved a success only less absolute than this, more than a few times in the course of his works. And it should be remembered always that poetry in any other sense than the sense of invention or divination, creation by dint of recollection and by force of reproduction, was by no means the aim and end of his ambition. The grace, the charm, the magic of poetry was to him always a secondary if not always an inconsiderable quality in comparison with the weight of matter, the solidity of meaning, the significance and purpose of the thing suggested or presented. The famous men whose names may most naturally and most rationally be coupled with the more illustrious name of Ben Jonson came short of the triumph which might have been theirs in consequence of their worst faults or defects—of the weaker and baser elements in their moral nature; because they preferred self-interest in the one case and self-indulgence in the other to the noble toil and the noble pleasure of doing their best for their art's sake and their duty's, to the ultimate satisfaction of their conscience; a guide as sure and a monitor as exacting in æsthetic matters—or, to use a Latin rather than a Greek word, in matters of pure intelligence—as in questions of ethics or morality. But with Ben Jonson conscience was the first and last consideration : the conscience of power which undoubtedly made him arrogant and exacting made him even more severe in self-exaction, more resolute in self-discipline, more inexorable in self-devotion to the elected labour of his life. From others he exacted much ; but less than he exacted from himself. And it is to this noble uprightness of mind, to this lofty loyalty in labour, that the gravest vices and the most serious defects of his work may indisputably be traced. Reversing the famous axiom of Goldsmith's professional art-critic, we may say of Jonson's work in almost every instance that the picture would have been better if the artist had taken less pains. For in some cases at least he writes better as soon as he allows himself to write with ease—or at all events without elaborate ostentation of effort and demonstrative prodigality of toil. The unequalled breadth and depth of his reading could not but enrich as well as encumber his writings : those who could wish he had been less learned may be reminded how much we should certainly lose—how much of solid and precious metal—for the mere chance of a possible gain in spontaneity and ease ; in qualities of lyrical or dramatic excellence which it is doubtful whether he had received from nature in any degree comparable with those to which his learning gave a fresh impulse and a double force of energetic life. And when his work is at its worst, when his faults are most flagrant, when his tediousness is most unendurable, it is not his learning that is to blame, for his learning is not even apparent. The obtrusion and accumulation of details and references, allusions and citations, which encumber the text and the margin of his first Roman tragedy with such a ponderous mass of illustrative superfluity, may undoubtedly be set down, if not to the discredit, at least to the disadvantage of the poet whose resolute caprice had impelled him to be author and commentator, dramatist and scholiast, at once : but however tedious a languid or a cursory reader may find this part of Jonson's work, he must, if not abnormally perverse in stupidity, admit that it is far less wearisome, less vexatious, less deplorable and insufferable, than the interminable deserts of dreary dialogue in which the affectations, pretentions, or idiocies of the period are subjected to the indefatigable and the lamentable industry of a caricaturist or a photographer.

There is nothing accidental in the work of Ben Jonson : no casual inspiration, no fortuitous impulse, ever guides or misguides his genius aright or astray. And this crowning and damning defect of a tedious and intolerable realism was even exceptionally wilful and premeditated. There is little if anything of it in the earliest comedy admitted into the magnificent edition which was compiled and published by himself in the year of the death of Shakespeare. And the humours of a still earlier comedy attributed to his hand, *The Case* and printed apparently without his sanc- *is Altered.* tion just seven years before, are not worked out with such wearisome patience nor exhibited with such scientific persistency as afterwards distinguished the anatomical lecturer on vice and folly whose ideal of comic art was a combination of sarcasm and sermon in alternately epigrammatic and declamatory dialogue. I am by no means disposed to question the authenticity of this play, an excellent example of romantic comedy dashed with farce and flavoured with poetry : but, as far as I am aware, no notice has yet been taken of a noticeable coincidence between the manner or the circum-

stances of its publication and that of a spurious
play which had nine years previously been attributed to Shakespeare.   Some copies only of *The
Case is Altered* bear on the title-page the name of
Jonson, as some copies only of *Sir John Oldcastle*
bear on the title-page the name of Shakespeare.
In the earlier case, there can of course be no
reasonable doubt that Shakespeare on his side, or
the four actual authors of the gallimaufry on theirs,
or perhaps all five together in the common though
diverse interest of their respective credits, must
have interfered to put a stop to the piratical profits
of a lying and thieving publisher by compelling
him to cancel the impudently mendacious title-
page which imputed to Shakespeare the authorship
of a play announced in its very prologue as the
work of a writer or writers whose intention was to
counteract the false impression given by Shakespeare's caricature, and to represent Prince Hal's old
lad of the castle in his proper character of hero and
martyr.   In the later case, there can be little if any
doubt that Jonson, then at the height of his fame
and influence, must have taken measures to pre-
clude the circulation under his name of a play which
he would not or could not honestly acknowledge.
So far, then, as external evidence goes, there is no

ground whatever for a decision as to whether *The Case is Altered* may be wholly or partially or not at all assignable to the hand of Jonson.   My own conviction is that he certainly had a hand in it, and was not improbably its sole author : but that on the other hand it may not impossibly be one of the compound works on which he was engaged as a dramatic apprentice with other and less energetic playwrights in the dim back workshop of the slave-dealer and slave-driver whose diary records the grinding toil and the scanty wages of his lean and laborious bondsmen.   Justice, at least since the days of Gifford, has generally been done to the bright and pleasant quality of this equally romantic and classical comedy ; in which the passionate humour of the miser is handled with more freshness and freedom than we find in most of Jonson's later studies, while the figure of his putative daughter has more of grace and interest than he usually vouchsafed to be at the pains of bestowing on his official heroines.   It is to be regretted, it is even to be deplored, that the influence of Plautus on the style and the method of Jonson was not more permanent and more profound.   Had he been but content to follow his first impulse, to work after his earliest model—had he happily preferred those 'Plautinos et numeros et sales' for which his courtly friend Horace expressed so courtierly a contempt to the heavier numbers and the more laborious humours which he set himself to elaborate and to cultivate instead, we might not have had to applaud a more wonderful and admirable result, we should unquestionably have enjoyed a harvest more spontaneous and more gracious, more generous and more delightful. Something of the charm of Fletcher, his sweet straightforward fluency and instinctive lightness of touch, would have tempered the severity and solidity of his deliberate satire and his heavy-handed realism.

And the noble work of comic art which followed on this first attempt gave even fuller evidence in its earlier than its later form of the author's capacity for poetic as well as realistic success. The defence of poetry which appears only in the first edition of *Every Man in his Humour* is worth all Sidney's and all Shelley's treatises thrown together. A stern and austere devotion to the principle which prohibits all indulgence in poetry, precludes all exuberance of expression, and immolates on the altar of accuracy all eloquence, all passion, and all inspiration incompatible with direct and prosaic reproduc-

EveryMan in his Humour.

tion of probable or plausible dialogue, induced its author to cancel this noble and majestic rhapsody ; and in so doing gave fair and full forewarning of the danger which was to beset this too rigid and conscientious artist through the whole of his magnificent career.   But in all other points the process of transformation to which its author saw fit to subject this comedy was unquestionably a process of improvement.   Transplanted from the imaginary or fantastic Italy in which at first they lived and moved and had their being to the actual and immediate atmosphere of contemporary London, the characters gain even more in lifelike and interesting veracity or verisimilitude than in familiar attraction and homely association.   Not only do we feel that we know them better, but we perceive that they are actually more real and cognisable creatures than they were under their former conditions of dramatic existence.   But it must be with regret as well as with wonder that we find ourselves constrained to recognize the indisputable truth that this first acknowledged work of so great a writer is as certainly his best as it certainly is not his greatest.   Never again did his genius, his industry, his conscience and his taste unite in the triumphant presentation of a work so faultless, so satisfactory, so absolute in achievement and so free from blemish or defect. The only three others among all his plays which are not unworthy to be ranked beside it are in many ways more wonderful, more splendid, more incomparable with any other product of human intelligence or genius : but neither *The Fox*, *The Alchemist*, nor *The Staple of News*, is altogether so blameless and flawless a piece of work ; so free from anything that might as well or better be dispensed with, so simply and thoroughly compact and complete in workmanship and in result. Molière himself has no character more exquisitely and spontaneously successful in presentation and evolution than the immortal and inimitable Bobadil : and even Bobadil is not unworthily surrounded and supported by the many other graver or lighter characters of this magnificent and perfect comedy.

It is difficult to attempt an estimate of the next endeavours or enterprises of Ben Jonson without incurring either the risk of impatient and uncritical injustice, if rein be given to the natural irritation and vexation of a disappointed and bewildered reader, or the no less imminent risk of one-sided and one-eyed partiality, if the superb literary quality, the elaborate intellectual excellence, of these undramatic if not inartistic satires in dialogue be duly taken into account. From their author's point of view, they are worthy of all the applause he claimed for them ; and to say this is to say much ; but if the author's point of view was radically wrong, was fundamentally unsound, we can but be divided between condemnation and applause, admiration and regret. No student of our glorious language, no lover of our glorious literature, can leave these miscalled comedies unread without foregoing an experience which he should be reluctant to forego : but no reader who has any sense or any conception of comic art or of dramatic harmony will be surprised to find that the author's experience of their reception on the stage should have driven him by steady gradations of fury and consecutive degrees of arrogance into a state of mind and a style of work which must have seemed even to his well-wishers most unpromising for his future and final triumph. Little if anything can be added to the excellent critical remarks of Gifford on *Every Man out of his Humour*, *Cynthia's Revels*, and *Poetaster, or his Arraignment*. The first of these magnificent mistakes would be enough to ensure immortality to the genius of the poet capable of so superb and

elaborate an error. The fervour and intensity of
the verse which expresses his loftier mood of
Every   intolerant indignation, the studious and
Man out
of his   implacable versatility of scorn which ani-
Humour.   mates the expression of his disgust at the
viler or crueller examples of social villainy then open
to his contemptuous or furious observation, though
they certainly cannot suffice to make a play, suffice
to make a living and imperishable work of the
dramatic satire which passes so rapidly from one
phàse to another of folly, fraud, or vice. And if it
were not an inadmissible theory that the action or
the structure of a play might be utterly disjointed
and dislocated in order to ensure the complete
presentation or development, the alternate exhibition or exposure, of each figure in the revolving
gallery of a satirical series, we could hardly fear
that our admiration of the component parts which
fail to compose a coherent or harmonious work of
art could possibly carry us too far into extravagance of applause. The noble rage which inspires
the overture is not more absolute or perfect than
the majestic structure of the verse : and the best
comic or realistic scenes of the ensuing play are
worthy to be compared—though it may not be
altogether to their advantage—with the similar

work of the greatest succeeding artists in narrative
or dramatic satire. Too much of the studious
humour, too much of the versatile and laborious
realism, displayed in the conduct and evolution of
this satirical drama, may have been lavished and
misused in the reproduction of ephemeral affectations and accidental forms of folly : but whenever
the dramatic satirist, on purpose or by accident,
strikes home to some deeper and more durable subject of satire, we feel the presence and the power
of a poet and a thinker whose genius was not born
to deal merely with ephemeral or casual matters.
The small patrician fop and his smaller plebeian
ape, though even now not undiverting figures, are
inevitably less diverting to us, as they must have
been even to the next generation from Jonson's,
than to the audience for whom they were created :
but the humour of the scene in which the highly
intelligent and intellectual lady, who regards herself as the pattern at once of social culture and
of personal refinement, is duped and disgraced by
an equally simple and ingenious trick played off
on her overweening and contemptuous vanity,
might have been applauded by Shakespeare or
by Vanbrugh, approved by Congreve or Molière.
Here, among too many sketches of a kind which

can lay claim to no merit beyond that of an
unlovely photograph, we find a really humorous
conception embodied in a really amusing type of
vanity and folly ; and are all the more astonished
to find a writer capable of such excellence and
such error as every competent reader must recognize in the conception and execution of this rather
admirable than delightful play.   For Molière himself could hardly have improved on the scene in
which a lady who is confident of her intuitive
capacity to distinguish a gentleman from a pre-
tender with no claim to that title is confronted
with a vulgar clown, whose introducers have
assured her that he is a high-bred gentleman mas-
querading for a wager under that repulsive likeness.
She wonders that they can have imagined her so
obtuse, so ignorant, so insensible to the difference
between gentleman and clown : she finds that he
plays his part as a boor very badly and trans-
parently ; and on discovering that he is in fact the
boor she would not recognize, is driven to vanish
in a passion of disgust.   This is good comedy :
but we can hardly say as much for the scene in
which a speculator who has been trading on the
starvation or destitution of his neighbours and
tenants is driven to hang himself in despair at the

tidings of a better market for the poor, is cut down
by the hands of peasants who have not recognized
him, and on hearing their loudly expressed regrets
for this act of inadvertent philanthropy becomes
at once a beneficent and penitent philanthropist.
Extravagant and exceptional as is this instance
of Jonson's capacity for dramatic error—for the
sacrifice at once of comic art and of common sense
on the altar of moral or satirical purpose, it is but
an extreme example of the result to which his
theory must have carried his genius, gagged and
handcuffed and drugged and blindfolded, had not
his genius been too strong even for the force and
the persistence of his theory. No reader and no
spectator of his next comedy can have been inclined
to believe or encouraged in believing
that it was. The famous final verse of the *Cynthia's Revels.*
epilogue to *Cynthia's Revels* can hardly
sound otherwise to modern ears than as an expression of blustering diffidence—of blatant self-distrust.
That any audience should have sat out the five
undramatic acts of this 'dramatic satire' is as inconceivable as that any reader, however exasperated
and exhausted by its voluminous perversities,
should fail to do justice to its literary merits; to
the vigour and purity of its English, to the mas-

culine refinement and the classic straightforward-
ness of its general style. There is an exquisite
song in it, and there are passages—nay, there are
scenes—of excellent prose : but the intolerable
elaboration of pretentious dullness and ostentatious
ineptitude for which the author claims not merely
the tolerance or the condonation which gratitude
or charity might accord to the misuse or abuse of
genius, but the acclamation due to its exercise and
the applause demanded by its triumph—the heavy-
headed perversity which ignores all the duties and
reclaims all the privileges of a dramatic poet—the
Cyclopean ponderosity of perseverance which
hammers through scene after scene at the task of
ridicule by anatomy of tedious and preposterous
futilities—all these too conscientious outrages
offered to the very principle of comedy, of poetry,
or of drama, make us wonder that we have no record of a retort from the exhausted audience—if
haply there were any auditors left—to the dogged
defiance of the epilogue :—

> By God 'tis good, and if you like 't you may.
> —By God 'tis bad, and worse than tongue can say.

For the most noticeable point in this studiously
wayward and laboriously erratic design is that the
principle of composition is as conspicuous by its

absence as the breath of inspiration : that the artist, the scholar, the disciple, the student of classic models, is as indiscoverable as the spontaneous humourist or poet. The wildest, the roughest, the crudest offspring of literary impulse working blindly on the passionate elements of excitable ignorance was never more formless, more incoherent, more defective in structure, than this voluminous abortion of deliberate intelligence and conscientious culture.

There is a curious monotony in the variety — if there be not rather a curious variety in the monotony—of character and of style which makes it even more difficult to resume the study of *Cynthia's Revels* when once broken off than even to read through its burdensome and bulky five acts at a sitting ; but the reader who lays siege to it with a sufficient supply of patience will find that the latter is the surer if not the only way to appreciate the genuine literary value of its better portions. Most of the figures presented are less than sketches and little more than outlines of inexpert and intolerant caricature : but the 'half-saved' or (as Carlyle has it) 'insalvable' coxcomb and parasite Asotus, who puts himself under the tuition of Amorphus and the patronage of Anaides, is a creature with something of real comic life in him. By what process of induction or deduction the wisdom of critical interpreters should have discerned in the figure of his patron, a fashionable ruffler and ruffian, the likeness of Thomas Dekker, a humble, hard-working, and highly-gifted hack of letters, may be explicable by those who can explain how the character of Hedon, a courtly and voluptuous coxcomb, can have been designed to cast ridicule on John Marston, a rude and rough-hewn man of genius, the fellow-craftsman of Ben Jonson as satirist and as playwright. But such absurdities of misapplication and misconstruction, once set afloat on the Lethean waters of stagnating tradition, will float for ever by grace of the very rottenness which prevents them from sinking. Ignorance assumes and idleness repeats what sciolism ends by accepting as a truth no less indisputable than undisputed. To any rational and careful student it must be obvious that until the publication of Jonson's *Poetaster* we cannot trace, I do not say with any certainty of evidence, but with any plausibility of conjecture, the identity of the principal persons attacked or derided by the satirist. And to identify the originals of such figures as Clove and Orange in *Every Man out of his Humour* can hardly, as Carlyle might have expressed it, be matter of serious interest to any son of Adam. But the famous polemical comedy which appeared a year later than the appearance of *Cynthia's Revels* bore evidence about it, unmistakable by reader or spectator, alike *Poetaster.* to the general design of the poet and to the particular direction of his personalities. Jonson of course asserted and of course believed that he had undergone gross and incessant provocation for years past from the 'petulant' onslaughts of Marston and Dekker : but what were his grounds for this assertion and this belief we have no means whatever of deciding—we have no ground whatever for conjecture. What we cannot but perceive is the possibly more important fact that indignation and ingenuity, pugnacity and self-esteem, combined to produce and succeeded in producing an incomparably better comedy than the author's last and a considerably better composition than the author's penultimate attempt. Even the 'apologetical dialogue' appended for the benefit of the reader, fierce and arrogant as it seems to us in its bellicose ambition and its quarrelsome self-assertion, is less violent and overweening in its tone than the furious eloquence of the prelude to

Every Man out of his Humour. The purity of passion, the sincerity of emotion, which inspires and inflames that singular and splendid substitute for an ordinary prologue, never found again an expression so fervent and so full in the many and various appeals of its author to his audience, immediate or imaginary, against the malevolence of enemies or of critics. But in this Augustan satire his rage and scorn are tempered and adapted to something of dramatic purpose ; their expression is more coherent, if not less truculent,—their effect is more harmonious, if not more genuine,—than in the two preceding plays.

There is much in the work of Ben Jonson which may seem strange and perplexing to the most devout and rapturous admirer of his genius : there is nothing so singular, so quaint, so inexplicable, as his selection of Horace for a sponsor or a patron saint. The affinity between Virgil and Tennyson, between Shelley and Lucretius, is patent and palpable : but when Jonson assumes the mask of Horace we can only wonder what would have been the sensation on Olympus if Pluto had suddenly proposed to play the part of Cupid, or if Vulcan had obligingly offered to run on the errands of Mercury. This eccentricity of egoism

is only less remarkable than the mixture of care
and recklessness in the composition of a play
which presents us at its opening with an apparent
hero in the person, not of Horace, but of Ovid;
and after following his fortunes through four-fifths
of the action, drops him into exile at the close of
the fourth act, and proceeds with the business of
the fifth as though no such figure had ever taken
part in the conduct of the play.   Shakespeare,
who in Jonson's opinion 'wanted art,' assuredly
never showed himself so insensible to the natural
rules of art as his censor has shown himself here.
Apart from the incoherence of construction which
was perhaps inevitable in such a complication of
serious with satirical design, there is more of
artistic merit in this composite work of art than
in any play produced by its author since the
memorable date of *Every Man in his Humour*.
The character of Captain Pantilius Tucca, which
seems to have brought down on its creator such
a boiling shower-bath or torrent of professional
indignation from quarters in which his own distinguished service as a soldier and a representative
champion of English military hardihood would
seem to have been unaccountably if not scandalously forgotten, is beyond comparison the

brightest and the best of his inventions since the
date of the creation of Bobadil. But the decrease
in humanity of humour, in cordial and genial
sympathy or tolerance of imagination, which
marks the advance of his genius towards its
culmination of scenical and satirical success in
The Alchemist must be obvious at this stage of his
work to those who will compare the delightful
cowardice and the inoffensive pretention of Bobadil
with the blatant vulgarity and the flagrant rascality of Tucca.

In the memorable year which brought into
England her first king of Scottish birth, and made
inevitable the future conflict between the revolu-
tionary principle of monarchy by divine right and
the conservative principle of self-government by
deputy for the commonweal of England, the first
great writer who thought fit to throw in his lot
with the advocates of the royalist revolution produced on the boards a tragedy of which
Sejanus.
the moral, despite his conscious or unconscious efforts to disguise or to distort it, is as
thoroughly republican and as tragically satirical
of despotism as is that of Shakespeare's *Julius
Cæsar*. It would be well for the fame of Jonson
if the parallel could be carried further : but,

although *Sejanus his Fall* may not have received
on its appearance the credit or the homage due
to the serious and solid merit of its composition
and its execution, it must be granted that the
author has once more fallen into the excusable
but nevertheless unpardonable error of the too
studious and industrious Martha. He was careful
and troubled about many things absolutely superfluous and supererogatory ; matters of no value
or concern whatever for the purpose or the import
of a dramatic poem : but the one thing needful, the
very condition of poetic life and dramatic interest,
he utterly and persistently overlooked. Tiberius, the
central character of the action—for the eponymous
hero or protagonist of the play is but a crude study
of covetous and lecherous ambition,— has not life
enough in the presentation of him to inform the
part with interest. No praise—of the sort which
is due to such labours—can be too high for the
strenuous and fervid conscience which inspires
every line of the laborious delineation : the recorded words of the tyrant are wrought into the
text, his traditional characteristics are welded into
the action, with a patient and earnest fidelity
which demands applause no less than recognition :
but when we turn from this elaborate statue—

from this exquisitely articulated skeleton—to the living figure of Octavius or of Antony, we feel and understand more than ever that Shakespeare 'hath chosen the good part, which shall not be taken away from him.'

Coleridge has very justly animadverted on 'the anachronic mixture' of Anglican or Caledonian royalism with the conservatism of an old Roman republican in the character of Arruntius : but we may trace something of the same incongruous combination in the character of a poet who was at once the sturdiest in aggressive eagerness of self-assertion, and the most copious in courtly effusion of panegyric, among all the distinguished writers of his day. The power of his verse and the purity of his English are nowhere more remarkable than in his two Roman tragedies : on the other hand, his great fault or defect as a dramatist is nowhere more perceptible. This general if not universal infirmity is one which never seems to have occurred to him, careful and studious though he was always of his own powers and performances, as anything of a fault at all. It is one indeed which no writer afflicted with it could reasonably be expected to recognize or to repair. Of all purely negative faults, all sins of intellectual omission, it is perhaps the most serious and the most irremediable. It is want of sympathy ; a lack of cordial interest, not in his own work or in his own genius,—no one will assert that Jonson was deficient on that score,—but in the individual persons, the men and women represented on the stage. He took so much interest in the creations that he had none left for the creatures of his intellect or art. This fault is not more obvious in the works of his disciples Cartwright and Randolph than in the works of their master. The whole interest is concentrated on the intellectual composition and the intellectual development of the characters and the scheme. Love and hatred, sympathy and antipathy, are superseded and supplanted by pure scientific curiosity : the clear glow of serious or humorous emotion is replaced by the dry light of analytical investigation. *Si vis me flere* — the proverb is something musty. Neither can we laugh heartily or long where all chance of sympathy or cordiality is absolutely inconceivable. The loving laughter which salutes the names of Dogberry and Touchstone, Mrs. Quickly and Falstaff, is never evoked by the most gorgeous opulence of humour, the most glorious audacity of intrigue, which dazzles and delights our understanding in the parts of Sir Epicure Mammon, Rabbi Zeal-of-the-Land Busy, Morose and Fitz-dottrel and Mosca: even Bobadil, the most comically attractive of all cowards and braggarts on record, has no such hold on our regard as many a knave and many a fool of Shakespeare's comic progeny. The triumph of 'Don Face' over his confederates, though we may not be so virtuous as to grudge it him, puts something of a strain upon our conscience if it is heartily to be applauded and enjoyed. One figure, indeed, among all the multitude of Jonson's invention, is so magnificent in the spiritual stature of his wickedness, in the still dilating verge and expanding proportion of his energies, that admiration in this single case may possibly if not properly overflow into something of intellectual if not moral sympathy. The genius and the courage of Volpone, his sublimity of cynic scorn and his intensity of contemptuous enjoy-ment,—his limitless capacity for pleasure and his dauntless contemplation of his crimes,—make of this superb sinner a figure which we can hardly realize without some sense of imperious fascination. His views of humanity are those of Swift and of Carlyle : but in him their fruit is not bitterness of sorrow and anger, but rapture of satisfaction

and of scorn. His English kinsman, Sir Epicure
Mammon, for all his wealth of sensual imagination
and voluptuous eloquence, for all his living play of
humour and glowing force of faith, is essentially
but a poor creature when set beside the great
Venetian. Had the study of Tiberius been in-
formed and vivified by something of the same
fervour, the tragedy of *Sejanus* might have had
in it some heat of more than merely literary life.
But this lesser excellence, the merit of vigorous
and vigilant devotion or application to a high and
serious object of literary labour, is apparent in
every scene of the tragedy. That the subject is
one absolutely devoid of all but historical and
literary interest—that not one of these scenes can
excite for one instant the least touch, the least
phantom, the least shadow of pity or terror—
would apparently have seemed to its author no
argument against its claim to greatness as a tragic
poem. But if it could be admitted, as it will never
be by any unperverted judgment, that this eternal
canon of tragic art, the law which defines terror
and pity as its only proper objects, the alpha and
omega of its aim and its design, may ever be
disregarded or ignored, we should likewise have to
admit that Jonson had in this instance achieved

a success as notable as we must otherwise consider his failure. For the accusation of weakness in moral design, of feeble or unnatural treatment of character, cannot with any show of justice be brought against him. Coleridge, whose judgment on a question of ethics will scarcely be allowed to carry as much weight as his authority on matters of imagination, objects with some vehemence to the incredible inconsistency of Sejanus in appealing for a sign to the divinity whose altar he proceeds to overthrow, whose power he proceeds to defy, on the appearance of an unfavourable presage. This doubtless is not the conduct of a strong man or a rational thinker : but the great minister of Tiberius is never for an instant throughout the whole course of the action represented as a man of any genuine strength or any solid intelligence. He is shown to us as merely a cunning, daring, unscrupulous and imperious upstart, whose greed and craft, impudence and audacity, intoxicate while they incite and undermine while they uplift him.

The year which witnessed the appearance of *Sejanus* on the stage—acclaimed by Chapman at greater length if not with greater fervour than by any other of Jonson's friends or satellites—

witnessed also the first appearance of its author in a character which undoubtedly gave free play to some of his most remarkable abilities, but which unquestionably diverted and distorted and absorbed his genius as a dramatist and his talent as a poet after a fashion which no capable student can contemplate without admiration or consider without regret. The few *Part of King James's Entertainment.* readers whose patient energy and conscientious curiosity may have led them to traverse—a pilgrimage more painful than Dante's or than Bunyan's—the entire record of the ' Entertainment ' which escorted and delayed, at so many successive stations, the progress through London and Westminster of the long-suffering son of Mary Queen of Scots, will probably agree that of the two poetic dialogues or eclogues contributed by Jonson to the metrical part of the ceremony, the dialogue of the Genius and the Flamen is better than that of the Genius and Thamesis ; more smooth, more vigorous, and more original. The subsequent prophecy of Electra is at all points unlike the prophecies of a Cassandra : there is something doubly tragic in the irony of chance which put into the mouth of Agamemnon's daughter a prophecy of good fortune to the royal house of Stuart on its first entrance

into the capital and ascension to the throne of England. The subsequent *Panegyre* is justly *A Pane-* praised by Gifford for its manly and dig-
gyre. nified style of official compliment—court-liness untainted by servility: but the style is rather that of fine prose, sedately and sedulously measured and modulated, than that of even ceremonial poetry.

In the same energetic year of his literary life the Laureate produced one of his best
The Satyr. minor works—*The Satyr*, a little lyric drama so bright and light and sweet in fancy and in finish of execution that we cannot grudge the expenditure of time and genius on so slight a sub-
The ject. *The Penates*, which appeared in
Penates. the following year, gave evidence again of the strong and lively fancy which was to be but too often exercised in the same field of in-genious and pliant invention. The metre is well conceived and gracefully arranged, worthy indeed of nobler words than those which it clothes with light and pleasant melody. The octosyllabics, it will be observed by metrical students, are certainly good, but decidedly not faultless: the burlesque part sustained by Pan is equally dexterous and brilliant in execution.

In 1605 the singular and magnificent coalition of powers which served to build up the composite genius of Jonson displayed in a single *Volpone, or The Fox.* masterpiece the consummate and crowning result of its marvellous energies. No other of even his very greatest works is at once so admirable and so enjoyable. The construction or composition of *The Alchemist* is perhaps more wonderful in the perfection and combination of cumulative detail, in triumphant simplicity of process and impeccable felicity of result : but there is in *Volpone* a touch of something like imagination, a savour of something like romance, which gives a higher tone to the style and a deeper interest to the action. The chief agents are indeed what Mr. Carlyle would have called ' unspeakably unexemplary mortals ' : but the serious fervour and passionate intensity of their resolute and resourceful wickedness give somewhat of a lurid and distorted dignity to the display of their doings and sufferings, which is wanting to the less gigantic and heroic villainies of Subtle, Dol, and Face. The absolutely unqualified and unrelieved rascality of every agent in the later comedy—unless an exception should be made in favour of the unfortunate though enterprising Surly—is another note of inferiority ; a mark of

comparative baseness in the dramatic metal. In
Volpone the tone of villainy and the tone of virtue
are alike higher. Celia is a harmless lady, if a too
submissive consort ; Bonario is an honourable
gentleman, if too dutiful a son. The Puritan and
shopkeeping scoundrels who are swindled by Face
and plundered by Lovewit are viler if less villainous
figures than the rapacious victims of Volpone.

As to the respective rank or comparative excellence of these two triumphant and transcendent
masterpieces, the critic who should take upon himself to pass sentence or pronounce judgment would
in my opinion display more audacity than discre-
tion. The steadfast and imperturbable skill of
hand which has woven so many threads of incident,
so many shades of character, so many changes of
intrigue, into so perfect and superb a pattern of incomparable art as dazzles and delights the reader
of *The Alchemist* is unquestionably unique—above
comparison with any later or earlier example of
kindred genius in the whole range of comedy, if
not in the whole world of fiction. The manifold
harmony of inventive combination and imaginative
contrast—the multitudinous unity of various and
concordant effects—the complexity and the
simplicity of action and impression, which hardly

allow the reader's mind to hesitate between enjoyment and astonishment, laughter and wonder,
admiration and diversion—all the distinctive
qualities which the alchemic cunning of the poet
has fused together in the crucible of dramatic satire
for the production of a flawless work of art, have
given us the most perfect model of imaginative
realism and satirical comedy that the world has
ever seen ; the most wonderful work of its kind
that can ever be run upon the same lines. Nor is
it possible to resist a certain sense of immoral
sympathy and humorous congratulation, more keen
than any Scapin or Mascarille can awake in the
mind of a virtuous reader, when Face dismisses
Surly with a promise to bring him word to his
lodging if he can hear of 'that Face' whom Surly
has sworn to mark for his if ever he meets him.
From the date of Plautus to the date of Sheridan it
would surely be difficult to find in any comedy a
touch of glorious impudence which might reasonably
be set against this. And the whole part is so full
of brilliant and effective and harmonious touches or
strokes of character or of humour that even this
crowning instance of serene inspiration in the line
of superhuman audacity seems merely right and
simply natural.

And yet, even while possessed and overmastered by the sense of the incomparable energy, the impeccable skill, and the indefatigable craftsmanship, which combined and conspired together to produce this æsthetically blameless masterpiece, the reader whose instinct requires something more than merely intellectual or æsthetic satisfaction must recognize even here the quality which distinguishes the genius of Ben Jonson from that of the very greatest imaginative humourists—Aristophanes or Rabelais, Shakespeare or Sterne, Vanbrugh or Dickens, Congreve or Thackeray. Each of these was evidently capable of falling in love with his own fancy—of rejoicing in his own imaginative humour as a swimmer in the waves he plays with : but this buoyant and passionate rapture was controlled by an instinctive sense which forbade them to strike out too far or follow the tide too long. However quaint or queer, however typical or exceptional, the figure presented may be— Olivia's or Tristram Shandy's uncle Toby, Sir John Brute or Mr. Peggotty, Lady Wishfort or Lady Kew,—we recognize and accept them as lifelike and actual intimates whose acquaintance has been made for life. Sir Sampson Legend might undoubtedly find himself as much out of place in the drawing-

room of the Countess Dowager of Kew as did Sir
Wilful Witwoud, on a memorable occasion, in the
saloon of his aunt Lady Wishfort: Captain Toby
Shandy could hardly have been expected to
tolerate the Rabelaisian effervescences of Sir Toby
Belch: and Vanbrugh's typical ruffians of rank
have little apparently in common with Dickens's
representative heroes of the poor. But in all these
immortal figures there is the lifeblood of eternal
life which can only be infused by the sympathetic
faith of the creator in his creature—the breath
which animates every word, even if the word be
not the very best word that might have been found,
with the vital impulse of infallible imagination.
But it is difficult to believe that Ben Jonson can
have believed, even with some half sympathetic and
half sardonic belief, in all the leading figures of his
invention. Scorn and indignation are but too often
the motives or the mainsprings of his comic art;
and when dramatic poetry can exist on the sterile
and fiery diet of scorn and indignation, we may
hope to find life sustained in happiness and health
on a diet of aperients and emetics. The one great
modern master of analytic art is somewhat humaner
than Jonson in the application of his scientific
method to the purpose of dramatic satire. The

study of Sludge is finer and subtler by far than the
study of Subtle ; though undoubtedly it is, in consequence of that very perfection and sublimation
of exhaustive analysis, less available for any but a
monodramatic purpose. No excuse, no plea, no
pretext beyond the fact of esurience and the sense
of ability, is suggested for the villainy of Subtle,
Dol, and Face. But if we were to see what might
possibly be said in extenuation of their rogueries,
to hear what might possibly be pleaded in explanation or condonation of their lives, the comedy
would fall through and go to pieces : the dramatic
effect would collapse and be dissolved. And to
this great, single, æsthetic end of art the consummate and conscientious artist who created these
immortal figures was content to subdue or to
sacrifice all other and subordinate considerations.
Coleridge, as no reader will probably need to be
reminded, 'thought the *Œdipus Tyrannus*, *The
Alchemist*, and *Tom Jones*, the three most perfect
plots ever planned.' With the warmest admiration
and appreciation of Fielding's noble and immortal
masterpiece, I cannot think it at all worthy of comparison, for blameless ingenuity of composition and
absolute impeccability of design, with the greatest
of tragic and the greatest of comic triumphs in

construction ever accomplished by the most consummate and the most conscientious among ancient
and modern artists. And when we remember that
this perfection of triumphant art is exhibited, not
on the scale of an ordinary comedy, whether classic
or romantic, comprising a few definite types and a
few impressive situations, but on a scale of invention
so vast and so various as to comprise in the course
of a single play as many characters and as many incidents, all perfectly adjusted and naturally developed
out of each other, as would amply suffice for the
entire dramatic furniture, for the entire poetic equip-
ment, of a great dramatic poet, we feel that Gifford's
expression, a 'prodigy of human intellect,' is equally
applicable to *The Fox* and to *The Alchemist*, and is
not a whit too strong a term for either. Nor can I
admit, as I cannot discern, the blemish or imper-
fection which others have alleged that they descry
in the composition of *Volpone*—the unlikelihood of
the device by which retribution is brought down in
the fifth act on the criminals who were left at the
close of the fourth act in impregnable security and
triumph. So far from regarding the comic Nemesis
or rather Ate which infatuates and impels Volpone
to his doom as a sacrifice of art to morality, an
immolation of probability and consistency on the

altar of poetic justice, I admire as a master-stroke of character the haughty audacity of caprice which produces or evolves his ruin out of his own hardihood and insolence of exulting and daring enjoyment. For there is something throughout of the lion as well as of the fox in this original and incomparable figure. I know not where to find a third instance of catastrophe comparable with that of either *The Fox* or *The Alchemist* in the whole range of the highest comedy; whether for completeness, for propriety, for interest, for ingenious felicity of event or for perfect combination and exposition of all the leading characters at once in supreme simplicity, unity, and fullness of culminating effect.

And only in the author's two great farces shall we find so vast a range and variety of characters. The foolish and famous couplet of doggrel rhyme which brackets *The Silent Woman* with *The Fox* and *The Alchemist* is liable to prejudice the reader against a work which if compared with those marvellous masterpieces must needs seem to lose its natural rights to notice, to forfeit its actual claim on our rational admiration. Its proper place is not with these, but beside its fellow example of exuberant, elaborate, and deliberately farcical realism—*Bartholomew Fair*. And the two are not less wonderful in their own way, less triumphant on their own lines, than those two crowning examples of comedy. Farcical in construction and in action, they belong to the province of the higher form of art by virtue of their leading characters. Morose indeed, as a victimized monomaniac, is rather a figure of farce than of comedy: Captain Otter and his termagant are characters of comedy rather broad than high: but the collegiate ladies, in their matchless mixture of pretention and profligacy, hypocrisy and pedantry, recall rather the comedies than the farces of Molière by the elaborate and vivid precision of portraiture which presents them in such perfect finish, with such vigour and veracity of effect. Again, if *Bartholomew Fair* is mere farce in many of its minor characters and in some of its grosser episodes and details, the immortal figure of Rabbi Busy belongs to the highest order of comedy. In that absolute and complete incarnation of Puritanism full justice is done to the merits while full justice is done upon the demerits of the barbarian sect from whose inherited and infectious tyranny this nation is as yet but imperfectly delivered. Brother Zeal-of-the-Land is no vulgar impostor, no mere religious quacksalver of such a kind as supplies the common food for satire, the common fuel of ridicule : he is a hypocrite of the earnest kind, an Ironside among civilians ; and the very abstinence of his creator from Hudibrastic misrepresentation and caricature makes the satire more thoroughly effective than all that Butler's exuberance of wit and prodigality of intellect could accomplish. The snuffling glutton who begins by exciting our laughter ends by displaying a comic perversity of stoicism in the stocks which is at least more respectable if not less laughable than the complacency of Justice Overdo, the fatuity of poor Cokes, the humble jocosity of a Littlewit, or the intemperate devotion of a Waspe. Hypocrisy streaked with sincerity, greed with a cross of earnestness and craft with a dash of fortitude, combine to make of the Rabbi at once the funniest, the fairest, and the faithfullest study ever taken of a less despicable than detestable type of fanatic.

Not only was the genius of Jonson too great, but his character was too radically noble for a realist or naturalist of the meaner sort. It is only in the minor parts of his gigantic work, only in its insignificant or superfluous components or details, that we find a tedious insistence on wearisome or offensive topics of inartistic satire or ineffectual display. Nor is it upon the ignoble sides of character that this great satiric dramatist prefers to concentrate his attention. As even in the most terrible masterpieces of Balzac, it is not the wickedness of the vicious or criminal agents, it is their energy of intellect, their dauntless versatility of daring, their invincible fertility of resource, for which our interest is claimed or by which our admiration is aroused. In Face as in Subtle, in Volpone as in Mosca, the qualities which delight us are virtues misapplied : it is not their cunning, their avarice, or their lust, it is their courage, their genius, and their wit in which we take no ignoble or irrational pleasure. And indeed it would be strange and incongruous if a great satirist who was also a great poet had erred so grossly as not to aim at this result, or had fallen so grievously short of his aim as not to vindicate the dignity of his design. The same year in which the stage first echoed the majestic accents of Volpone's opening speech was distinguished by the appearance of the *Masque of Blackness* : a work eminent even among its author's in splendour of fancy, invention, and flowing eloquence. Its companion or counterpart, the *Masque of Beauty*, a poem even more notable

The Masque of Blackness.

The Masque of Beauty.

for these qualities than its precursor, did not appear till three years later. Its brilliant and picturesque variations on the previous theme afford a perfect example of poetic as distinct from prosaic ingenuity.

Between the dates of these two masques, which were first printed and published together, three other entertainments had employed the energetic genius of the Laureate on the double task of scenical invention and literary decoration. The first occasion was that famous visit of King Christian and his hard-drinking Danes which is patriotically supposed to have done so much harm to the proverbially sober and abstemious nation whose temperance is so vividly depicted by the enthusiastic cordiality of Iago. The *Enter-*

Entertainment of Two Kings at Theobalds.

tainment of Two Kings at Theobalds opens well, with two vigorous and sonorous couplets of welcome : but the Latin verses are hardly worthy of Gifford's too fervid commendation. The mock marriage of the boyish Earl of Essex and the girl afterwards known to ill

Hymenaei.

fame as Countess of Somerset gave occasion of which Jonson availed himself to the full for massive display of antiquarian magnificence and indefatigable prodigality of inexhaustible detail. The epithalamium of these quasi-nuptials is fine—when it is not coarse (we cannot away, for instance, with the comparison, in serious poetry, of kisses to—cockles !) : but the exuberant enthusiasm of Gifford for 'this chaste and beautiful gem' is liable to provoke in the reader's mind a comparison 'with the divine original' : and among the very few poets who could sustain a comparison with Catullus no man capable of learning the merest rudiments of poetry will affirm that Ben Jonson can be ranked. His verses are smooth and strong, 'well-torned and true-filed' : but the matchless magic, the impeccable inspiration, the grace, the music, the simple and spontaneous perfection of the Latin poem, he could pretend neither to rival nor to reproduce. 'What was my part,' says Jonson in a note, 'the faults here, as well as the virtues, must speak.' These are the concluding words of a most generous and cordial tribute to the merits of the mechanist or stage-carpenter, the musician, and the dancing-master—Inigo Jones, Alfonso Ferrabosco, and Thomas Giles—who were employed on the composition of this magnificent if ill-omened pageant : and they may very reasonably be applied to the two translations from Catullus which the poet— certainly no prophet on this particular occasion—thought fit to introduce into the ceremonial verse of the masques held on the first and second nights of these star-crossed festivities. The faults and the virtues, the vigour of phrase and the accuracy of rendering, the stiffness of expression and the slowness of movement, are unmistakably characteristic of the workman. But in the second night's masque it must be noted that the original verse is distinctly better than the translated stanzas : the dispute of Truth and Opinion is a singularly spirited and vigorous example of amœbæan allegory. In the next year's

Entertain- ment of King James and Queen Anne at Theobalds. *Entertainment* of the king and queen at Theobalds, then ceded by its owner to the king, the happy simplicity of invention and arrangement is worthily seconded or supported by the grave and dignified music of the elegiac verse which welcomes the coming and speeds the parting master. Next year *The Masque of Beauty* and the masque at Lord Haddington's marriage, each containing some of Jonson's finest and most flowing verse, bore equal witness to the energy and to the elasticity of his genius for apt and varied invention. The amœbæan stanzas in the later of these two masques have more freedom of movement and spontaneity of music than will perhaps be found in any other poem of equal length from the same indefatigable hand. The fourth of these stanzas is *Masque at* simply magnificent : the loveliness of the *Lord Haddington's* next is impaired by that anatomical par- *Marriage.* ticularity which too often defaces the serious verse of Jonson with grotesque if not gross deformity of detail. No other poet, except possibly one of his spiritual sons, too surely 'sealed of the tribe of Ben,' would have introduced 'liver' and 'lights' into a sweet and graceful effusion of lyric fancy, good alike in form and sound ; a commendation not always nor indeed very frequently deserved by the verse of its author. The variations in the burden of 'Hymen's war' are singularly delicate and happy.

The next was a memorable year in the literary life of Ben Jonson : it witnessed the appearance both of the magnificent *Masque* *The* *of Queens* and of the famous comedy or *Masque of* farce of *The Silent Woman.* The mar- *Queens.* vellously vivid and dexterous application of marvellous learning and labour which distinguishes the most splendid of all masques as one of the typically splendid monuments or trophies of English literature has apparently eclipsed, in the appreciation of the general student, that equally admirable fervour of commanding fancy which informs the whole design and gives life to every detail. The interlude of the witches is so royally lavish in its wealth and variety of fertile and lively horror that on a first reading the student may probably do less than justice to the lofty and temperate eloquence of the noble verse and the noble prose which follow.

Of *The Silent Woman* it is not easy to say anything new and true. Its merits are salient *The Silent* and superb: the combination of parts *Woman.* and the accumulation of incidents are so skilfully arranged and so powerfully designed that the result is in its own way incomparable —or comparable only with other works of the master's hand while yet in the fullness of its cunning and the freshness of its strength. But a play of this kind must inevitably challenge a comparison, in the judgment of modern readers, between its author and Molière: and Jonson can hardly, on the whole, sustain that most perilous comparison. It is true that there is matter enough in Jonson's play to have furnished forth two or three of Molière's: and that on that ground—on the score of industrious intelligence and laborious versa-

tility of humour—*The Silent Woman* is as superior
to the *Misanthrope* and the *Bourgeois Gentilhomme*
as to *Twelfth Night* and *Much Ado about Nothing*.
But even when most dazzled by the splendour of
studied wit and the felicity of deliberate humour
which may even yet explain the extraordinary
popularity or reputation of this most imperial and
elaborate of all farces, we feel that the author
could no more have rivalled the author of *Twelfth
Night* than he could have rivalled the author of
Othello. The Nemesis of the satirist is upon him :
he cannot be simply at ease : he cannot be happy
in his work without some undertone of sarcasm,
some afterthought of allusion, aimed at matters
which Molière would have reserved for a slighter
style of satire, and which Shakespeare would
scarcely have condescended to recognise as possible
objects of even momentary attention. His wit is
wonderful—admirable, laughable, laudable—it is
not in the fullest and the deepest sense delightful.
It is radically cruel, contemptuous, intolerant :
the sneer of the superior person—Dauphine or
Clerimont—is always ready to pass into a snarl :
there is something in this great classic writer of
the bull-baiting or bear-baiting brutality of his
age. We put down *The Fox* or *The Alchemist*

with a sense of wondering admiration, hardly affected by the impression of some occasional superfluity or excess: we lay aside *The Silent Woman*, not indeed without grateful recollection of much cordial enjoyment, but with distinct if reluctant conviction that the generous table at which we have been so prodigally entertained was more than a little crowded and overloaded with multifarious if savoury encumbrance of dishes. And if, as was Gifford's opinion, Shakespeare took a hint from the mock duellists in this comedy for the mock duellists in *Twelfth Night*, how wonderfully has he improved on his model! The broad rude humour of Jonson's practical joke is boyishly brutal in the horseplay of its violence : the sweet bright fun of Shakespeare's is in perfect keeping with the purer air of the sunnier climate it thrives in. The divine good-nature, the godlike good-humour of Shakespeare can never be quite perfectly appreciated till we compare his playfulness or his merriment with other men's. Even that of Aristophanes seems to smack of the barbarian beside it.

I cannot but fear that to thorough-going Jonsonians my remarks on the great comedy in which Dryden found the highest perfection of dramatic art on record may seem inadequate if not inappreciative. But to do it anything like justice would take up more space than I can spare : it would indeed, like most of Jonson's other successful plays, demand a separate study of some length and elaboration. The high comedy of the collegiate ladies, the low comedy of Captain and Mrs. Otter, the braggart knights and the Latinist barber, are all as masterly as the versions of Ovid's elegiacs into prose dialogue are tedious in their ingenuity and profitless in their skill. As to the chief character—who must evidently have been a native of Ecclefechan—he is as superior to the *malade imaginaire*, or to any of the Sganarelles of Molière, as is Molière himself to Jonson in lightness of spontaneous movement and easy grace of inspiration. And this is perhaps the only play of Jonson's which will keep the reader or spectator for whole scenes together in an inward riot or an open passion of subdued or unrepressed laughter.

The speeches at Prince Henry's Barriers, written by the Laureate for the occasion of the heir apparent's investiture as Prince of Wales, are noticeable for their fine and dexterous fusion of legend with history in eloquent and weighty verse. But the *Masque of Oberon*, presented the day before

The Speeches at Prince Henry's Barriers.

the tournament in which the prince bore himself so gallantly as to excite ' the great wonder of the beholders,' is memorable for a quality far
The Masque of Oberon. higher than this : it is unsurpassed if not unequalled by any other work of its author for brightness and lightness and grace of fancy, for' lyric movement and happy simplicity of expression.

Such work, however, was but the byplay in which the genius of this indefatigable poet found its natural relaxation during the year
The Alchemist. which gave to the world for all time a gift so munificent as that of *The Alchemist.* This ' unequalled play,' as it was called by contemporary admirers, was not miscalled by their enthusiasm ; it is in some respects un- paralleled among all the existing masterpieces of comedy.   No student worthy of the name who may agree with me in preferring *The Fox* to *The Alchemist* will wish to enforce his pre- ference upon others.   Such perfection of plot, with such multiplicity of characters—such in- genuity of incident, with such harmony of construc- tion—can be matched, we may surely venture to say, nowhere in the whole vast range of comic inven- tion—nowhere in the whole wide world of dramatic fiction.   If the interest is less poignant than in

Volpone, the fun less continuous than in *The Silent Woman*, the action less simple and spontaneous than that of *Every Man in his Humour*, the vein of comedy is even richer than in any of these other masterpieces. The great Sir Epicure is enough in himself to immortalize the glory of the great artist who conceived and achieved a design so fresh, so daring, so colossal in its humour as that of this magnificent character. And there are at least nine others in the play as perfect in drawing, as vivid in outline, as living in every limb and every feature, as even his whose poetic stature overtops them all. The deathless three confederates, Kastrill and Surly, Dapper and Drugger, the too perennial Puritans whose villainous whine of purity and hypocrisy has its living echoes even now—not a figure among them could have been carved or coloured by any other hand.

Nor is the list even yet complete of Jonson's poetic work during this truly wonderful year of his literary life. At Christmas he produced ' the Queen's Majesty's masque ' of *Love freed from Ignorance and Folly* ; a little *Love freed from Igno- rance and Folly.* dramatic poem composed in his lightest and softest vein of fancy, brilliant and melodious throughout. The mighty and majestic Poet Laureate would hardly, I fear, have accepted with benignity the tribute of a compliment to the effect that his use of the sweet and simple heptasyllabic metre was worthy of Richard Barnfield or George Wither : but it is certain that in purity and fluency of music his verse can seldom be compared, as here it justly may, with the clear flutelike notes of *Cynthia* and *The Shepherd's Hunting.* An absurd misprint in the last line but three has afflicted all Jonson's editors with unaccountable perplexity. 'Then, then, angry music sound,' sings the chorus at the close of a song in honour of 'gentle Love and Beauty.' It is inconceivable that no one should yet have discovered the obvious solution of so slight but unfortunate an error in the type as the substitution of 'angry' for 'airy.'

The tragedy of *Catiline his Conspiracy* gave evidence in the following year that the author of *Sejanus* could do better, but could not do much better, on the same rigid lines of rhetorical and studious work which he had followed in the earlier play. Fine as is the opening of this too laborious tragedy, the stately verse has less of dramatic movement than of such as might be proper —if such a thing could be—for epic satire cast into the form of dialogue. Catiline is so mere a monster

Catiline.

of ravenous malignity and irrational atrocity that he simply impresses us as an irresponsible though criminal lunatic : and there is something so preposterous, so abnormal, in the conduct and language of all concerned in his conspiracy, that nothing attributed to them seems either rationally credible or logically incredible. Coleridge, in his notes on the first act of this play, expresses his conviction that one passage must surely have fallen into the wrong place—such action at such a moment being impossible for any human creature. But the whole atmosphere is unreal, the whole action unnatural : no one thing said or done is less unlike the truth of life than any other : the writing is immeasurably better than the style of the ranting tragedian Seneca, but the treatment of character is hardly more serious as a study of humanity than his. In fact, what we find here is exactly what we find in the least successful of Jonson's comedies : a study, not of humanity, but of humours. The bloody humour of Cethegus, the braggart humour of Curius, the sluggish humour of Lentulus, the swaggering humour of Catiline himself—a huffcap hero as ever mouthed and strutted out his hour on the stage—all these alike fall under the famous definition of his favourite phrase which the poet had given twelve years before in the induction to the second of his acknowledged comedies.   And a tragedy of humours is hardly less than a monster in nature—or rather in that art which 'itself is nature.' Otherwise the second act must be pronounced excellent : the humours of the rival harlots, the masculine ambition of Sempronia, the caprices and cajoleries of Fulvia, are drawn with Jonson's most self-conscious care and skill. But the part of Cicero is burden enough to stifle any play : and some even of the finest passages, such as the much-praised description of the dying Catiline, fine though they be, are not good in the stricter sense of the word ; the rhetorical sub-limity of their diction comes most perilously near the verge of bombast. Altogether, the play is another magnificent mistake : and each time we open or close it we find it more difficult to believe that the additions made by its author some ten years before to *The Spanish Tragedy* can possibly have been those printed in the later issues of that famous play.[1] Their subtle and

---

[1] No student will need to be reminded of what is apparently unknown to some writers who have thought fit to offer an opinion on this subject—that different additions were made at different dates, and by different hands, to certain popular plays of the time. The original *Faustus* of Marlowe was altered and re-altered, at least

spontaneous notes of nature, their profound and
searching pathos, their strange and thrilling tone of
reality, the beauty and the terror and the truth of
every touch, are the signs of a great, a very great
tragic poet : and it is all but unimaginable that
such an one could have been, but a year or so
afterwards, the author of *Sejanus*—and again, eight
years later, the author of *Catiline*. There is fine
occasional writing in each, but it is not dramatic :
and there is good dramatic work in each, but it is
not tragic.

For two years after the appearance of *Catiline*
there is an interval of silence and inaction in the
literary life of its author ; an intermission of labour
which we cannot pretend to explain in the case
of this Herculean workman, who seems usually to
have taken an austere and strenuous delight in
the employment and exhibition of his colossal
energies. His next work is one of which it seems
all but impossible for criticism to speak with
neither more nor less than justice. Gifford himself,
the most devoted of editors and of partisans, to

---

three times, by three if not more purveyors of interpolated and incongruous matter : and even that superb masterpiece would hardly
seem to have rivalled the popularity of Kyd's tragedy—a popularity
by no means unmerited.

whom all serious students of Jonson owe a tribute of gratitude and respect, seems to have wavered in his judgment on this point to a quite unaccountable degree. In his memoirs of Ben Jonson *Bartholomew Fair* is described as 'a popular piece, but chiefly remarkable for the obloquy to which it has given birth.' In his final note on the play, he expresses an opinion that it has 'not unjustly' been considered as 'nearly on a level with those exquisite dramas, *The Fox* and *The Alchemist*.' Who shall decide when not only do doctors disagree, but the most self-confident of doctors in criticism disagrees with himself to so singular an extent? The dainty palate of Leigh Hunt was naturally nauseated by the undoubtedly greasy flavour of the dramatic viands here served up in such prodigality of profusion : and it must be confessed that some of the meat is too high and some of the sauces are too rank for any but a very strong digestion. But those who turn away from the table in sheer disgust at the coarseness of the fare will lose the enjoyment of some of the richest and strongest humour, some of the most brilliant and varied realism, that ever claimed the attention or excited the admiration of the study or the stage. That

Bartholomew Fair.

'superlunatical hypocrite,' the immortal and only too immortal Rabbi Busy, towers above the minor characters of the play as the execrable fanaticism which he typifies and embodies was destined to tower above reason and humanity, charity and common sense, in its future influence on the social life of England. But in sheer force and fidelity of presentation this wonderful study from nature can hardly be said to exceed the others which surround and set it off; the dotard Littlewit, the booby Cokes, the petulant fidelity and pig-headed self-confidence of Waspe, the various humours and more various villainies of the multitudinous and riotous subordinates; above all, that enterprising and intelligent champion of social purity, the conscientious and clear-sighted Justice Adam Overdo. When all is said that can reasonably be said against the too accurate reproduction and the too voluminous exposition of vulgar and vicious nature in this enormous and multitudinous pageant—too serious in its satire and too various in its movement for a farce, too farcical in its incidents and too violent in its horseplay for a comedy—the delightful humour of its finer scenes, the wonderful vigour and veracity of the whole, the unsurpassed ingenuity and dexterity of the composition, the energy, harmony, and versatility of the action, must be admitted to ensure its place for ever among the minor and coarser masterpieces of comic art.

The masque of *Love Restored*, to which no date is assigned by the author or his editors, *Love Restored.* has some noticeable qualities in common with the play which has just been considered, and ought perhaps to have taken precedence of it in our descriptive catalogue. Robin Goodfellow's adventures at court are described with such realistic as well as fantastic humour that his narrative might have made part of the incidents or episodes of the Fair without any impropriety or incongruity; but the lyric fancy and the spirited allegory which enliven this delightful little miniature of a play make it more heartily and more simply enjoyable than many or indeed than most of its author's works. Three other masques were certainly produced during the course of the year 1614. *A Challenge at Tilt at a Marriage*, which was produced eight *A Challenge at Tilt at a Marriage.* years after the *Masque of Hymen*, opened the new year with a superb display in honour of the second nuptials of the lady whose previous marriage, now cancelled as a nullity,

had been acclaimed by the poet with such
superfluous munificence of congratulation and of
augury as might have made him hesitate, or at
least might make us wish that he had seen fit to
hesitate, before undertaking the celebration of the
bride's remarriage—even had it not been made
infamously memorable by association with matters
less familiar to England at any time than to Rome
under Pope Alexander VI. or to Paris under
Queen Catherine de' Medici. But from the literary
point of view, as distinguished from the ethical or
the historical, we have less reason to regret than
to rejoice in so graceful an example of the poet's
abilities as a writer of bright, facile, ingenious
and exquisite prose. *The Irish Masque,* *The Irish*
presented four days later, may doubtless *Masque.*
have been written with no sarcastic intention ;
but if there was really no such under-current
of suggestion or intimation designed or imagined by the writer, we can only find a still
keener savour of satire, a still clearer indication of
insight, in the characteristic representation of a
province whose typical champions fall to wrangling
and exchange of reciprocal insults over the display
of their ruffianly devotion : while there is not
merely a tone of official rebuke or courtly compli-

ment, but a note of genuine good feeling and serious good sense, in the fine solid blank verse delivered by 'a civil gentleman of the nation.'

Mercury Vindicated from the Alche- mists. On Twelfth Night the comic masque of *Mercury Vindicated from the Alchemists* gave evidence that the creator of Subtle had not exhausted his arsenal of ridicule, but had yet some shafts of satire left for the professors of Subtle's art or mystery. The humour here is somewhat elaborate, though unquestionably spirited and ingenious.

The next year's is again a blank record; but the year 1616, though to us more mournfully memorable for the timeless death of Shakespeare, is also for the student of Ben Jonson a date of exceptional importance and interest. The pro- duction of two masques and a comedy in verse, with the publication of the magnificent first edition of his collected plays and poems, must have kept his name more continuously if not more vividly before the world than in any preceding year of his literary life. The masque of *The Golden Age Restored*, presented on New Year's Night and again on Twelfth Night, is equally ingenious and equally spirited in its happy simplicity of construction and in the vigorous

fluency of its versification ; which is generally
smooth, and in the lyrical dialogue from after the
first dance to the close may fairly be called sweet ;
an epithet very seldom applicable to the solid
and polished verse of Jonson. And if *The Devil
is an Ass* cannot be ranked among the crowning masterpieces of its author, it is not *The Devil
is an Ass.*
because the play shows any sign of
decadence in literary power or in humorous invention : the writing is admirable, the wealth of
comic matter is only too copious, the characters
are as firm in outline and as rich in colour as any
but the most triumphant examples of his satirical
or sympathetic skill in finished delineation and
demarcation of humours. On the other hand, it
is of all Ben Jonson's comedies since the date of
Cynthia's Revels the most obsolete in subject of
satire, the most temporary in its allusions and
applications : the want of fusion or even connection
(except of the most mechanical or casual kind)
between the various parts of its structure and the
alternate topics of its ridicule makes the action
more difficult to follow than that of many more
complicated plots : and, finally, the admixture of
serious sentiment and noble emotion is not so

skilfully managed as to evade the imputation of incongruity. Nevertheless, there are touches in the dialogue between Lady Tailbush and Lady Eitherside in the first scene of the fourth act which are worthy of Molière himself, and suggestive of the method and the genius to which we owe the immortal enjoyment derived from the society of Cathos and Madelon—I should say, Polixène and Aminte, of Célimène and Arsinoé, and of Phila-minte and Bélise. The third scene of the same act is so nobly written that the reader may feel half inclined to condone or to forget the previous humiliation of the too compliant heroine—her ser-vile and undignified submission to the infamous imbecility of her husband—in admiration of the noble and natural eloquence with which the poet has here endowed her. But this husband, comical as are the scenes in which he develops and dilates from the part of a dupe to the part of an impostor, is a figure almost too loathsome to be ludicrous — or at least, however ludicrous, to be fit for the leading part in a comedy of ethics as well as of manners. And the prodigality of elaboration lavished on such a multitude of subordinate cha-racters, at the expense of all continuous interest and to the sacrifice of all dramatic harmony, may tempt the reader to apostrophize the poet in his own words :—

> You are so covetous still to embrace
> More than you can, that you lose all.

Yet a word of parting praise must be given to Satan : a small part as far as extent goes, but a splendid example of high comic imagination after the order of Aristophanes, admirably relieved by the low comedy of the asinine Pug and the voluble doggrel of the antiquated Vice.

Not till nine years after the appearance of this play, in which the genius of the author may be said—in familiar phraseology—to have fallen between two stools, carrying either too much suggestion of human interest for a half allegorical satire, or not enough to give actual interest to the process of the satirical allegory, did Ben Jonson produce on the stage a masterpiece of comedy in which this danger was avoided, this difficulty overcome, with absolute and triumphant facility of execution. In the meantime, however, he had produced nine masques—or ten, counting that which appeared in the same year with his last great work of comic art. The *Masque* *The Masque of Christmas.* *of Christmas*, which belongs to the same year as the two works last mentioned, is a com-

fortable little piece of genial comic realism ; pleasant, quaint, and homely : the good-humoured
humour of little Robin Cupid and his honest old
mother 'Venus, a deaf tirewoman,' is more agreeable than many more studious and elaborate
examples of the author's fidelity as a painter or
photographer of humble life.   Next year, in the
Lovers   masque of *Lovers made Men*, called by
made Men.   Gifford *The Masque of Lethe*, he gave full
play to his lighter genius and lyric humour : it
is a work of exceptionally simple, natural, and
graceful fancy.   In the following year he brought
The Vision out the much-admired *Vision of Delight* ;
of Delight. a very fair example of his capacities
and incapacities.   The fanciful, smooth, and flowing verse of its graver parts would be worthy of
Fletcher, were it not that the music is less fresh
and pure in melody, and that among the finest
and sweetest passages there are interspersed such
lamentably flat and stiff couplets as would have
been impossible to any other poet of equal rank.
If justice has not been done in modern times to Ben
Jonson as one of the greatest of dramatists and
humourists, much more than justice has been done
to him as a lyric poet.   The famous song of Night in
this masque opens and closes most beautifully and

most sweetly : but two out of the eleven lines which compose it, the fifth and the sixth, are positively and intolerably bad. The barbarous and pedantic license of inversion which disfigures his best lyrics with such verses as these—'Create of airy forms a stream,' 'But might I of Jove's nectar sup'—is not a fault of the age but a vice of the poet. Marlowe and Lyly, Shakespeare and Webster, Fletcher and Dekker, could write songs as free from this blemish as Tennyson's or Shelley's. There is no surer test of the born lyric poet than the presence or absence of an instinctive sense which assures him when and how and where to use or to abstain from inversion. And in Jonson it was utterly wanting.

The next year's masque, *Pleasure Reconciled to Virtue*, would be very graceful in composition if it were not rather awkward in construction. *Pleasure Reconciled to Virtue.* The verses in praise of dancing are very pretty, sedate, and polished: and the burlesque part (spoken by 'Messer Gaster' in person) has more than usual of Rabelaisian freedom and energy. The antimasque afterwards prefixed to it, *For the Honour of Wales*, is somewhat *For the Honour of Wales.* ponderous in its jocularity, but has genuine touches of humour and serious notes of character in its 'tedious and brief' display of the poet's incomparable industry and devotion to the study of dialects and details : and the close is noble and simple in its patriotic or provincial eloquence. But in the year 1620 the comic genius of Jonson shone out once more in all the splendour

News from the New World discovered in the Moon.

of its strength. The only masque of that year, *News from the New World discovered in the Moon*, is worthy of a prose Aristophanes : in other words, it is a satire such as Aristophanes might have written, if that greater poet had ever condescended to write prose. Here for once the generous words of Jonson's noble panegyric on Shakespeare may justly be applied to himself : in his own immortal phrase, the humour of this little comedy is ' not of an age, but for all time.' At the very opening we find ourselves on but too familiar ground, and feel that the poet must have shot himself forward by sheer inspiration into our own enlightened age, when we hear 'a printer of news ' avowing the notable fact that ' I do hearken after them, wherever they be, at any rates ; I'll give anything for a good copy now, be it true or false, so it be news.' Are not these, the reader must ask himself, the accents of some gutter gaolbird—some dunghill gazetteer of this very present day ? Or is the avowal too honest in its impudence for such

lips as these? After this, the anticipation of something like railways ('coaches' that 'go only with
wind')—if not also of something like balloons
('a castle in the air that runs upon wheels, with a
winged lanthorn')—seems but a commonplace example of prophetic instinct.

The longest of Ben Jonson's masques was ex-
panded to its present bulk by the additions made
at each successive representation before the king;
to whose not over delicate or fastidious taste this
Masque of the Metamorphosed Gipsies
would seem to have given incomparable if *A Masque of the Metamorphosed Gipsies.*
not inexhaustible delight. And even those
readers who may least enjoy the decidedly
greasy wit or humour of some among its once most
popular lyrical parts must admire and cannot but
enjoy the rare and even refined loveliness of others.
The fortune most unfortunately told of his future
life and death to the future King Charles I. is told
in the very best lyric verse that the poet could
command: a strain of quite exceptional sweetness,
simplicity, and purity of music: to which, as we
read it now, the record of history seems to play a
most tragically ironical accompaniment, in a minor
key of subdued and sardonic presage. And besides
these graver and lovelier interludes of poetry which

relieve the somewhat obtrusive realism of the broader comic parts, this masque has other claims on our notice and remembrance; the ingenuity and dexterity, the richness of resource and the pliability of humour, which inform and animate all its lyric prophecies or compliments.

The masque which appeared in the following year is a monument of learning and labour such as

The Masque of Augurs. no other poet could have dreamed of lavishing on a ceremonial or official piece of work, and which can only be appreciated by careful reading and thorough study of the copious notes and references appended to the text. But the writer's fancy was at a low ebb when it could devise nothing better than is to be found in this *Masque of Augurs*: the humour is coarse and clumsy, the verses are flat and stiff. In the next year's Twelfth-Night masque, *Time vindicated to himself and to his honours*, the vigorous

Time vindicated to himself and to his honours. and vicious personalities of the attack on George Wither give some life to the part in which the author of *Abuses Stript and Whipt* is brought in under the name of Chronomastix to make mirth for the groundlings of the Court. The feeble and facile fluency of his pedestrian Muse in the least fortunate hours of her too voluble and voluminous improvisation is not unfairly caricatured; but the Laureate's malevolence is something too obvious in his ridicule of the 'soft ambling verse' whose 'rapture' at its highest has the quality denied by nature to Jonson's—the divine gift of melodious and passionate simplicity. A better and happier use for his yet unimpaired faculty of humour was found in the following year's masque of *Neptune's Triumph for the Return of Albion*; which contains the most famous and eloquent panegyric on the art of cookery that ever anticipated the ardours of Thackeray and the enthusiasm of Dumas.

The passage is a really superb example of tragicomic or mock-heroic blank verse; and in the closing lyrics of the masque there is no lack of graceful fancy and harmonious *Neptune's Triumph for the Return of Albion.*

elegance. For the next year's masque of *Pan's Anniversary, or The Shepherd's Holiaay*, not quite so much can reasonably be said. It is a typical and a flagrant instance of the poet's proverbial and incurable tendency to overdo everything: there is but artificial smoothness in the verse, and but clownish ingenuity in the prose of it. *Pan's Anniversary.*

But the year 1625 is memorable to the students

and admirers of Ben Jonson for the appearance of a work worth almost all his masques together; a work in which the author of *The Fox* and *The Alchemist* once more reasserted his claim to a seat which no other poet and no other dramatist could dispute. The last complete and finished masterpiece of his genius is the splendid comedy of *The Staple of News.* This, rather than *The Silent Woman*, is the play which should be considered as the third—or perhaps we should say the fourth—of the crowning works which represent the consummate and incomparable powers of its author. No man can know anything worth knowing of Ben Jonson who has not studied and digested the text of *Every Man in his Humour*, *The Fox*, *The Alchemist*, and *The Staple of News*: but any man who has may be said to know him well. To a cursory or an incompetent reader it may appear at first sight that the damning fault of *The Devil is an Ass* is also the fault of this later comedy: that we have here again an infelicitous and an incongruous combination of realistic satire with Aristophanic allegory, and that the harmony of the different parts, the unity of the composite action, which a pupil of Aristophanes should at least have striven to attain—or, if he could not, at

least to imitate and to respect—can here be considered as conspicuous only by their absence.
But no careful and candid critic will retain such an
impression after due study has been given to the
third poetic comedy which reveals to us the genius
of Jonson, not merely as a realistic artist in prose
or a master of magnificent farce, but as a great
comic poet. The scheme of his last preceding
comedy had been vitiated by a want of coherence
between the actual and the allegorical, the fantastic
and the literal point of view ; and the result was
confusion without fusion of parts : here, on the
other hand, we have fusion without confusion
between the dramatic allegory suggested by Aristophanes, the admirably fresh and living presentation of the three Pennyboys, and the prophetic
satire of the newsmarket or Stock Exchange of
journalism. The competent reader will be divided
between surprise at the possibility and delight in
the perfection of the success achieved by a poet
who has actually endowed with sufficiency of comic
life and humorous reality a whole group of symbolic
personifications ; from the magnificent Infanta
herself, Aurelia Clara Pecunia, most gracious and
generous yet most sensitive and discreet of imperial
damsels, even down to little ' blushet ' Rose Wax

the chambermaid. Her young suitor is at least as
good a picture of a generous light-headed prodigal
as ever was shown on any stage : as much of a
man as Charles Surface, and very much more of a
gentleman. The miserly uncle, though very well
drawn, is less exceptionally well drawn : but
Pennyboy Canter, the disguised father, is equally
delightful from the moment of his entrance with
an extempore carol of salutation on his lips to
those in which he appears to rescue the misused
Infanta from the neglectful favourite of her choice,
and reappears at the close of the play to rescue his
son, redeem his brother, and scatter the community
of jeerers : to whose humour Gifford is somewhat
less than just when he compares it with 'the
vapouring in *Bartholomew Fair*' : for it is neither
coarse nor tedious, and takes up but very little
space ; and that not unamusingly. As for the
great scene of the Staple, it is one of the most
masterly in ancient or modern comedy of the
typical or satirical kind. The central 'Office'
here opened, to the great offence (it should seem)
of 'most of the spectators'—a fact which, as
Gifford justly remarks, 'argues very little for the
good sense of the audience,'—may be regarded by
a modern student as representing the narrow little

nest in which was laid the modest little egg of
modern journalism—that bird of many notes and
many feathers, now so like an eagle and now so
like a vulture : now soaring as a falcon or sailing
as a pigeon over continents and battle-fields, now
grovelling and groping as a dunghill kite, with its
beak in a very middenstead of falsehood and of
filth. The vast range of Ben Jonson's interest and
observation is here as manifest as the wide scope
and infinite variety of his humour. Science and
warfare, Spinola and Galileo, come alike within
reach of its notice, and serve alike for the material
of its merriment. The invention of torpedos is
anticipated by two centuries and a half; while in
the assiduity of the newsmongers who traffic in
eavesdropping detail we acknowledge a resem-
blance to that estimable race of tradesmen known to
Parisian accuracy as interwieveurs. And the lunacy
of apocalyptic interpreters or prophets is gibbeted
side by side with the fanatical ignorance of
missionary enthusiasm, with impostures of professional quackery and speculations in personal
libel. Certainly, if ever Ben deserved the prophetic
title of Vates, it was in this last magnificent work
of his maturest genius. Never had his style or his
verse been riper or richer, more vigorous or more

pure. And even the interludes in which we hear the commentary and gather the verdict of 'these ridiculous gossips' (as their creator calls them) 'who tattle between the acts' are incomparably superior to his earlier efforts or excursions in the same field of humorous invention. The intrusive commentators on *Every Man out of his Humour*, for instance, are mere nullities—the awkward and abortive issue of unconscious uneasiness and inartistic egoism. But Expectation, Mirth, Tattle, and Censure, are genuine and living sketches of natural and amusing figures: and their dialogues, for appropriate and spirited simplicity, are worthy of comparison with even those of a similar nature which we owe not more to the genius than to the assailants of Molière.

In 1625 Ben Jonson had brought out his last great comedy: in 1626 he brought out the last

The Masque of Owls.

The Fortunate Isles, and their Union.

of his finer sort of masques. The little so-called *Masque of Owls*, which precedes it in the table of contents, is (as Gifford points out) no masque at all: it is a quaint effusion of doggrel dashed with wit and streaked with satire. But in *The Fortunate Isles, and their Union*, the humour and the verse are alike excellent: the jest on

Plato's ideas would have delighted Landor, and
the wish of Merefool to 'see a Brahman or a
Gymnosophist' is worthy of a modern believer in
esoteric Buddhism. Few if any of the masques
have in them lyrics of smoother and clearer flow ;
and the construction is no less graceful than ingenious. The next reappearance of the poet, after
a silence during three years of broken or breaking
health, was so memorably unfortunate in its issue
that the name and the fate of a play which was
only too naturally and deservedly hooted off the
stage are probably familiar to many who know
nothing of the masterpiece which had last preceded
it. Ever since Lamb gathered some excerpts from
the more high-toned and elaborate passages *The New
of The New Inn, or The Light Heart,* *Inn.*
and commended in them 'the poetical fancy and
elegance of mind of the supposed rugged old bard,'
it has been the fashion to do justice if not something more than justice to the literary qualities of
this play ; which no doubt contains much vigorous
and some graceful writing, and may now and then
amuse a tolerant reader by its accumulating and
culminating absurdities of action and catastrophe,
character and event. But that the work shows
portentous signs of mental decay, or at all events

of temporary collapse in judgment and in sense, can be questioned by no sane reader of so much as the argument. To rank any preceding play of Jonson's among those dismissed by Dryden as his 'dotages' would be to attribute to Dryden a verdict displaying the veriest imbecility of impudence : but to *The New Inn* that rough and somewhat brutal phrase is on the whole but too plausibly applicable.

At the beginning of the next year Jonson came forward in his official capacity as court poet or *Love's Triumph through Callipolis.* laureate, and produced 'the Queen's Masque,' *Love's Triumph through Callipolis,* and again, at Shrovetide, 'the King's Masque,' *Chloridia.* A few good verses, faint echoes of a former song, redeem the first of these from the condemnation of compassion or contempt: and there is still some evidence in its composition of conscientious energy and of capacity not yet reduced from the stage of decadence to the stage of collapse. But the hymn which begins fairly enough with imitation of an earlier and nobler strain of verse at once subsides into commonplace, and closes in doggrel which would have disgraced a Sylvester *Chloridia.* or a Quarles. It is impossible to read *Chloridia* without a regretful reflection on the lapse of time which prevented it from being a beautiful and typical instance of the author's lyric power : but, however inferior it may be to what he would have made of so beautiful a subject in the freshness and fullness of his inventive and fanciful genius, it is still ingenious and effective after a fashion ; and the first song is so genuinely graceful and simple as to remind us of Wordsworth in his more pedestrian but not uninspired moods or measures of lyrical or elegiac verse.

The higher genius of Ben Jonson as a comic poet was yet once more to show itself in one brilliant flash of parting splendour before its approaching sunset. No other of his works would seem to have met with such all but universal neglect as *The Magnetic Lady* ; I do not remember to have ever seen it quoted *The Magnetic Lady.* or referred to, except once by Dryden, who in his *Essay of Dramatic Poesy* cites from it an example of narrative substituted for action, ' where one comes out from dinner, and relates the quarrels and disorders of it, to save the undecent appearance of them on the stage, and to abbreviate the story.' And yet any competent spectator of its opening scenes must have felt a keen satisfaction at the apparent revival of the comic power and renewal of the dramatic instinct so lamentably enfeebled and eclipsed on the last occasion of a new play from the same hand. The first act is full of brilliant satirical description and humorous analysis of humours : the commentator Compass, to whom we owe these masterly summaries of character, is an excellent counterpart of that 'reasonable man' who so constantly reappears on the stage of Molière to correct with his ridicule or control by his influence the extravagant or erratic tendencies of his associates. Very few examples of Jonson's grave and deliberate humour are finer than the ironical counsel given by Compass to the courtly fop whom he dissuades from challenging the soldier who has insulted him, on the ground that the soldier

> has killed so many
> As it is ten to one his turn is next :
> You never fought with any, less, slew any;
> And therefore have the [fairer] hopes before you.

The rest of the speech, with all that follows to the close of the scene, is no less ripe and rich in sedate and ingenious irony. There is no less admirable humour in the previous discourse of the usurer in praise of wealth—especially as being the only real test of a man's character :—

> For, be he rich, he straight with evidence knows
> Whether he have any compassion

Or inclination unto virtue, or no :
Where the poor knave erroneously believes
If he were rich he would build churches, or
Do such mad things.

Most of the characters are naturally and vigorously drawn in outline or in profile : Dame Polish is a figure well worthy the cordial and lavish commendation of Gifford : and the action is not only original and ingenious, but during the first four acts at any rate harmonious and amusing.   The fifth act seems to me somewhat weaker; but the interludes are full of spirit, good humour, and good sense.

A Tale of a Tub, which appeared in the following year, is a singular sample of farce elaborated and exalted into comedy.   This rustic *A Tale of* study, though 'not liked' by the king *a Tub.* and queen when acted before them at court, has very real merits in a homely way.   The list of characters looks unpromising, and reminds us to regret that the old poet could not be induced to profit by Feltham's very just and reasonable animadversions on 'all your jests so nominal'; which deface this play no less than *The New Inn*, and repel the most tolerant reader by their formal and laborious puerility.   But the action opens brightly and briskly : the dispute about 'Zin Valentine' is only less good in its way than one

of George Eliot's exquisite minor touches—Mr.
Dempster's derivation of the word Presbyterian
from one Jack Presbyter of historic infamy : the
young squire's careful and testy 'man and
governor' is no unworthy younger brother of
Numps in *Bartholomew Fair* : and the rustic
heroine, a figure sketched with rough realistic
humour, is hardly less than delightful when she
remarks, after witnessing the arrest of her intended
bridegroom on a charge of highway robbery, ' He
might have married one first, and have been
hanged after, if he had had a mind to 't ;' a reflection worthy of Congreve or Vanbrugh, Miss
Hoyden or Miss Prue.   But Jonson had never
laid to heart the wisdom expressed in the admirable proverb—' Qui trop embrasse mal étreint ;'
the simple subject of the play and the homely
motive of the action are overlaid and overloaded
by the multiplicity of minor characters and epi-
sodical superfluities, and the upshot of all the
poet's really ingenious contrivances is pointless as
well as farcical and flat as well as trivial.   But
there is certainly no sign of dotage in any work
of Ben Jonson's produced before or after the
lamentable date of *The New Inn*.   The author
apologizes for the homely and rustic quality of his

uncourtly play; but if it be a failure, it is not on account of its plebeian humility, but through the writer's want of any real sympathy with his characters, any hearty relish of his subject: because throughout the whole conduct of a complicated intrigue he shows himself ungenially observant and contemptuously studious of his models: because the qualities most needed for such work, transparent lucidity and straightforward simplicity of exposition, are not to be found in these last comedies: because, for instance, as much attention is needed to appreciate the ingenious process of 'humours reconciled' in *The Magnetic Lady*, or to follow the no less ingenious evolution of boorish rivalries and clownish intrigues in the play just noticed, as to follow the action and appreciate the design of *The Fox* or *The Alchemist*.

The masque of this year, *Love's Welcome at Welbeck*, is a thing of very slight pretentions, but not unsuccessful or undiverting after its homely fashion. In the next year's *Love's Welcome at Welbeck.* companion masque, *Love's Welcome at Bolsover*, the verse, though not wanting in *Love's Welcome at Bolsover.* grace or ease, is less remarkable than the rough personal satire on Inigo Jones; who, it may be observed, is as ready with a quotation from

Chaucer as Goody Polish in *The Magnetic Lady* or Lovel in *The New Inn*.

Of this great dramatist's other than dramatic work in poetry or in prose this is not the place to speak : and his two posthumous fragments of dramatic poetry, interesting and characteristic as they are, can hardly affect for the better or for the worse our estimate of his powers. Had *Mortimer his Fall* been completed, we should undoubtedly have had a third example of rhetorical drama, careful, conscientious, energetic, impassive and impressive ; worthy to stand beside the author's two Roman tragedies : and Mortimer might have confronted and outfaced Sejanus and Catiline in sonorous audacity of rhythmic self-assertion and triumphant ostentation of magnificent vacuity. In *The Sad Shepherd* we find the faults and the merits of his best and his worst masques so blended and confounded that we cannot but perceive the injurious effect on the Laureate's genius or instinct of intelligence produced by the habit of conventional invention which the writing of verse to order and the arrangement of effects for a pageant had now made inevitable and incurable. A masque including an antimasque, in which the serious part

Mortimer his Fall.

The Sad Shepherd.

is relieved and set off by the introduction of
parody or burlesque, was a form of art or artificial
fashion in which incongruity was a merit; the
grosser the burlesque, the broader the parody,
the greater was the success and the more effective
was the result: but in a dramatic attempt of
higher pretention than such as might be looked
for in the literary groundwork or raw material for
a pageant, this intrusion of incongruous contrast
is a pure barbarism—a positive solecism in composition. The collocation of such names and such
figures as those of Æglamour and Earine with
such others as Much and Maudlin, Scathlock and
Scarlet, is no whit less preposterous or less ridiculous, less inartistic or less irritating, than the
conjunction in Dekker's *Satiromastix* of Peter
Flash and Sir Quintilian, Sir Adam Prickshaft
and Sir Vaughan ap Rees, with Crispinus and
Demetrius, Asinius and Horace: and the offence
is graver, more inexcusable and more inexplicable,
in a work of pure fancy or imagination, than in a
work of poetic invention crossed and chequered
with controversial satire. Yet Gifford, who can
hardly find words or occasions sufficient to express
his sense of Dekker's 'inconceivable folly,' or his
contempt for 'a plot that can scarcely be equalled

in absurdity by the worst of the plays which Dekker was ever employed to "dress,"' has not a syllable of reprehension for the portentous incongruities of this mature and elaborate poem. On the other hand, even Gifford's editorial enthusiasm could not overestimate the ingenious excellence of construction, the masterly harmony of composition, which every reader of the argument must have observed with such admiration as can but intensify his regret that scarcely half of the projected poem has come down to us. No work of Ben Jonson's is more amusing and agreeable to read, as none is more nobly graceful in expression or more excellent in simplicity of style.

The immense influence of this great writer on his own generation is not more evident or more memorable than is the refraction or reverberation of that influence on the next. This 'sovereign sway and masterdom,' this overpowering preponderance of reputation, could not but be and could not but pass away. No giant had ever the divine versatility of a Shakespeare : but of all the giant brood none ever showed so much diversity of power as Jonson. In no single work has he displayed such masterly variety of style as has Byron in his two great poems, *Don Juan* and *The Vision*

of Judgment : the results of his attempts at mixture
or fusion of poetry with farce will stand exposed
in all their deformity and discrepancy if we set
them beside the triumphant results of Shakespeare's. That faultless felicity of divine caprice
which harmonizes into such absolute congruity
all the outwardly incompatible elements of such
works as *Twelfth Night* and *The Tempest*, the
Winter's Tale and *A Midsummer Night's Dream*,
is perhaps of all Shakespeare's incomparable gifts
the one most utterly beyond reach of other poets.
But when we consider the various faculties and
powers of Jonson's genius and intelligence, when
we examine severally the divers forces and capacities enjoyed and exercised by this giant workman in the performance of his work, we are
amazed into admiration only less in its degree
than we feel for the greatest among poets. It is
not admiration of the same kind : there is less in
it of love and worship than we give to the gods of
song ; but it is with deep reverence and with
glowing gratitude that we salute in this Titan of
the English stage 'il maestro di color che sanno.'

II. MISCELLANEOUS WORKS

II

MISCELLANEOUS WORKS

AMONG the great dramatic poets of the Shakespearean age there are several who would still
have a claim to enduring remembrance as poets,
even had they never written a line for the theatre :
there are two only who would hold a high rank
among the masters of English prose. For Nash
was not a poet or a dramatist who wandered
occasionally into prose by way of change or
diversion : he was a master of prose who strayed
now and then into lyric or dramatic verse. Hey-
wood, Middleton, and Ford have left us more or
less curious and valuable works in prose ; essays
and pamphlets or chronicles and compilations :
but these are works of historic interest rather than
literary merit ; or, if this be too strong and
sweeping an expression, they are works of less
intrinsic than empirical value. But if all his plays
were lost to us, the author of Ben Jonson's

Explorata, or Discoveries, would yet retain a seat among English prose-writers beside the author of Bacon's Essays : the author of *The Gull's Horn-book* and *The Bachelor's Banquet* would still stand high in the foremost rank of English humourists.

The book of epigrams published by Jonson in the collected edition of his select works up *Epigrams.* to the date of the year 1616 is by no means an attractive introduction or an alluring prelude to the voluminous collection of miscellanies which in all modern editions it precedes. ' It is to be lamented,' in Gifford's opinion, ' on many accounts,' that the author has not left ʌus ' a further selection.' It is in my opinion to be deplored that he should have left us so large a selection—if that be the proper term—as he has seen fit to bequeath to a naturally and happily limited set of readers. ' Sunt bona, sunt quædam mediocria, sunt mala plura ': and the worst are so bad, so foul if not so dull, so stupid if not so filthy, that the student stands aghast with astonishment at the self-deceiving capacity of a writer who could prefix to such a collection the vaunt that his book was ' not covetous of least self-fame '— ' much less ' prone to indulgence in ' beastly phrase.' No man can ever have been less amenable than Sir Walter Scott to the infamous charge of Puritanism or prudery; and it is he who has left on record his opinion that 'surely that coarseness of taste which tainted Ben Jonson's powerful mind is proved from his writings. Many authors of that age are indecent, but Jonson is filthy and gross in his pleasantry, and indulges himself in using the language of scavengers and nightmen.' I will only add that the evidence of this is flagrant in certain pages which I never forced myself to read through till I had undertaken to give a full and fair account—to the best of my ability—of Ben Jonson's complete works. How far poetry may be permitted to go in the line of sensual pleasure or sexual emotion may be debatable between the disciples of Ariosto and the disciples of Milton; but all English readers, I trust, will agree with me that coprology should be left to Frenchmen. Among them—that is, of course, among the baser sort of them—that unsavoury science will seemingly never lack disciples of the most nauseous, the most abject, the most deliberate bestiality. It is nothing less than lamentable that so great an English writer as Ben Jonson should ever have taken the plunge of a Parisian diver into the cesspool: but it is as necessary to register as it is natural to deplore the detestable fact that he did so. The collection of his epigrams which bears only too noisome witness to this fact is nevertheless by no means devoid of valuable and admirable components. The sixty-fifth, a palinode or recantation of some previous panegyric, is very spirited and vigorous; and the verses of panegyric which precede and follow it are wanting neither in force nor in point. The poem 'on Lucy Countess of Bedford,' for which Gifford seems hardly able to find words adequate to his admiration, would be worthy of very high praise if the texture of its expression and versification were unstiffened and undisfigured by the clumsy license of awkward inversions. *The New Cry*, a brief and brilliant satire on political gossips of the *gobemouche* order, has one couplet worthy of Dryden himself, descriptive of such pretenders to statecraft as

> talk reserved, locked up, and full of fear,
> Nay, ask you how the day goes, in your ear;
> *Keep a Star-chamber sentence close twelve days,*
> *And whisper what a Proclamation says.*

The epitaph on little Salathiel Pavy, who had acted under his own name in the induction to *Cynthia's Revels*, is as deservedly famous as any minor work of Jonson's ; for sweetness and simplicity it has few if any equals among his lyrical attempts.

Of the fifteen lyric or elegiac poems which compose *The Forest*, there is none that is not worthy of all but the highest praise ; *The Forest.* there is none that is worthy of the highest. To come so near so often and yet never to touch the goal of lyric triumph has never been the fortune and the misfortune of any other poet. Vigour of thought, purity of phrase, condensed and polished rhetoric, refined and appropriate eloquence, studious and serious felicity of expression, finished and fortunate elaboration of verse, might have been considered as qualities sufficient to secure a triumph for the poet in whose work all these excellent attributes are united and displayed ; and we cannot wonder that younger men who had come within the circle of his personal influence should have thought that the combination of them all must ensure to their possessor a place above all his possible compeers.   But among the humblest and most devout of these prostrate enthusiasts was one who had but to lay an idle and reckless hand on the instrument which hardly would answer the touch of his master's at all, and the very note of

lyric poetry as it should be—as it was in the
beginning, as it is, and as it will be for ever—
responded on the instant to the instinctive intelligence of his touch.   As we turn from Gray to
Collins, as we turn from Wordsworth to Coleridge,
as we turn from Byron to Shelley, so do we turn
from Jonson to Herrick ; and so do we recognize
the lyric poet as distinguished from the writer who
may or may not have every gift but one in higher
development of excellence and in fuller perfection
of power, but who is utterly and absolutely tran-
scended and shone down by his probably unconscious competitor on the proper and peculiar ground
of pure and simple poetry.

But the special peculiarity of the case now
before us is that it was so much the greater man
who was distanced and eclipsed ; and this not
merely by a minor poet, but by a humble admirer
and a studious disciple of his own.   Herrick, as a
writer of elegies, epithalamiums, panegyrical or
complimentary verses, is as plainly and as openly
an imitator of his model as ever was the merest
parasite of any leading poet, from the days of
Chaucer and his satellites to the days of Tennyson
and his.   No Lydgate or Lytton was ever more
obsequious in his discipleship ; but for all his

loving and loyal protestations of passionate humility and of ardent reverence, we see at every turn, at every step, at every change of note, that what the master could not do the pupil can. When Chapman set sail after Marlowe, he went floundering and lurching in the wake of a vessel that went straight and smooth before the fullest and the fairest wind of song; but when Herrick follows Jonson the manner of movement or the method of progression is reversed. Macaulay, in a well-known passage, has spoken of Ben Jonson's 'rugged rhymes'; but rugged is not exactly the most appropriate epithet. Donne is rugged: Jonson is stiff. And if ruggedness of verse is a damaging blemish, stiffness of verse is a destructive infirmity. Ruggedness is curable; witness Donne's *Anniversaries*: stiffness is incurable; witness Jonson's *Underwoods*. In these, as in the preceding series called *The Forest*, there is so lavish a display *Underwoods*. of such various powers as cannot but excite the admiration they demand and deserve. They have every quality, their author would undoubtedly have maintained, that a student of poetry ought to expect and to applaud. What they want is that magic without which the very best verse is as far beneath the very best prose as the verse

which has it is above all prose that ever was or ever can be written. And there never was a generation of Englishmen in which this magic was a gift so common as it was in Jonson's. We have but to open either of the priceless volumes which we owe to the exquisite taste and the untiring devotion of Mr. Bullen, and we shall come upon scores after scores of 'lyrics from Elizabethan song-books' as far beyond comparison with the very best of Jonson's as Shakespeare is beyond comparison with Shirley, as Milton is beyond comparison with Glover, or as Coleridge is beyond comparison with Southey. There is exceptional ease of movement, exceptional grace of expression, in the lyric which evoked from Gifford the 'free' avowal, 'if it be not the most beautiful song in the language, I know not, for my part, where it is to be found.' Who on earth, then or now, would ever have supposed that the worthy Gifford did? But any one who does know anything more of the matter than the satirist and reviewer whose own amatory verses were 'lazy as Scheldt and cold as Don' will acknow-ledge that it would be difficult to enumerate the names of poets contemporary with Jonson, from Frank Davison to Robin Herrick, who have left us songs at least as beautiful as that beginning—
'Oh do not wanton with those eyes, Lest I be sick

with seeing.' And in 'the admirable Epode,' as
Gifford calls it, which concludes Ben Jonson's
contributions to *Love's Martyr*, though there is
remarkable energy of expression, the irregularity
and inequality of style are at least as conspicuous
as the occasional vigour and the casual felicity of
phrase. But if all were as good as the best passages this early poem of Jonson's would undoubtedly be very good indeed. Take for instance
the description or definition of true love :

> That is an essence far more gentle, fine, [1]
>   Pure, perfect, nay divine ;
> It is a golden chain let down from heaven,
>   Whose links are bright and even,
> That falls like sleep on lovers.

Again :

> O, who is he that in this peace enjoys
>   The elixir of all joys,
> (A form more fresh than are the Eden bowers
>   And lasting as her flowers ;
> Richer than time, and as time's virtue rare,
>   Sober as saddest care,
> A fixed thought, an eye untaught to glance ;)
>   Who, blest with such high chance,
> Would at suggestion of a steep desire
>   Cast himself from the spire
> Of all his happiness ?

---

[1] In the original edition, 'most **gentile** and fine' : a curious
Italianism which must have seemed questionable or unallowable to
the author's maturer taste.

And few of Jonson's many moral or gnomic passages are finer than the following :

> He that for love of goodness hateth ill
>   Is more crown-worthy still
> Than he which for sin's penalty forbears;
>   His heart sins, though he fears.

This metre, though very liable to the danger of monotony, is to my ear very pleasant ; but that of the much admired and doubtless admirable address to Sir Robert Wroth is much less so. This poem is as good and sufficient an example of the author's ability and inability as could be found in the whole range of his elegiac or lyric works. It has excellent and evident qualities of style ; energy and purity, clearness and sufficiency, simplicity and polish ; but it is wanting in charm. Grace, attraction, fascination, the typical and essential properties of verse, it has not. Were Jonson to be placed among the gods of song, we should have to say of him what Æschylus says of Death—

> μόνου δὲ Πειθὼ δαιμόνων ἀποστατεῖ.

The spirit of persuasive enchantment, the goddess of entrancing inspiration, kept aloof from him alone of all his peers or rivals. To men far weaker, to poets not worthy to be named with him on the score of creative power, she gave the gift which from him was all but utterly withheld. And therefore it is that his place is not beside Shakespeare, Milton, or Shelley, but merely above Dryden, Byron, and Crabbe. The verses on Penshurst are among his best, wanting neither in grace of form nor stateliness of sound, if too surely wanting in the indefinable quality of distinction or inspiration : and the farewell to the world has a savour of George Herbert's style about it which suggests that the sacred poet must have been a sometime student of the secular. Beaumont, again, must have taken as a model of his lighter lyric style the bright and ringing verses on the proposition 'that women are but men's shadows.' The opening couplet of the striking address 'to Heaven' has been, it seems to me, misunderstood by Gifford ; the meaning is not—' Can I not think of God without its making me melancholy ? ' but 'Can I not think of God without its being imputed or set down by others to a fit of dejection ? ' The few sacred poems which open the posthumous collection of his miscellaneous verse are far inferior to the best of Herrick's *Noble Numbers* ; although the second of the three must probably have served the minor poet as an occasional model.

The *Celebration of Charis in ten lyric pieces* would be a graceful example of Jonson's lighter and brighter inspiration if the ten were reduced to eight. His anapæsts are actually worse than Shelley's : which hope would fain have assumed and charity would fain have believed to be impossible. 'We will take our plan from the new world of man, and our work shall be called the Pro-me-the-an '—even the hideous and excruciating cacophony of that horrible sentence is not so utterly inconceivable as verse, is not so fearfully and wonderfully immetrical as this : 'And from her arched brows such a grace sheds itself through the face.' The wheeziest of barrel-organs, the most broken-winded of bagpipes, grinds or snorts out sweeter melody than that. But the heptasyllabic verses among which this monstrous abortion rears its amorphous head are better than might have been expected ; not, as Gifford says of one example, ' above all praise,' but creditable at their best and tolerable at their worst.

The miscellaneous verses collected under the pretty and appropriate name of *Underwoods* comprise more than a few of Ben Jonson's happiest and most finished examples of lyric, elegiac, and gnomic or didactic poetry ; and likewise not a

little of such rigid and frigid work as makes us
regret the too strenuous and habitual application
of so devoted a literary craftsman to his professional round of labour. The fifth of these poems,
A Nymph's Passion, is not only pretty and ingenious, but in the structure of its peculiar stanza
may remind a modern reader of some among the
many metrical experiments or inventions of a
more exquisite and spontaneous lyric poet, Miss
Christina Rossetti. The verses ' on a lover's dust,
made sand for an hour-glass,' just come short of
excellence in their fantastic way; those on his
picture are something more than smooth and
neat; those against jealousy are exceptionally
sweet and spontaneous, again recalling the manner
of the poetess just mentioned ; with a touch of
something like Shelley's—

> I wish the sun should shine
> On all men's fruits and flowers, as well as mine—

and also of something like George Herbert's at
his best. *The Dream* is one of Jonson's most
happily inspired and most happily expressed
fancies; the close of it is for once not less than
charming.

Of the various elegies and epistles included in

this collection it need only be said that there is
much thoughtful and powerful writing in most if
not in all of them, with occasional phrases or
couplets of rare felicity, and here and there a
noble note of enthusiasm or a masterly touch of
satire. In the epistle to Sir Edward Sackvile the
sketch of the 'infants of the sword' who 'give
thanks by stealth' and in whispers for benefits
which they are ready to disown with imprecations
in public is worthy of the hand which drew
Bobadil and Tucca. The sonnet to Lady Mary
Wroth, good in itself, is characteristic in its
preference of the orthodox Italian structure to
the English or Shakespearean form. The four
very powerful and remarkable elegies on a lover's
quarrel and separation I should be inclined to
attribute rather to Donne than to Jonson; their
earnest passion, their quaint frankness, their verbal
violence, their eccentric ardour of expression, at
once unabashed and vehement, spontaneous and
ingenious, are all of them typical characteristics
of the future dean in the secular and irregular
days of his hot poetic youth. The fourth and
final poem of the little series is especially impressive and attractive. The turn of the sentences
and the cadence of the verse are no less significant

of the authorship than is a noble couplet in the poem immediately preceding them—which would at once be recognized by a competent reader as Jonson's :

> So may the fruitful vine my temples steep,
> And fame wake for me when I yield to sleep!

The 'epistle answering to one that asked to be sealed of the tribe of Ben' is better in spirit than in execution; manful, straightforward, and upright. The 'epigram' or rather satire 'on the Court Pucelle' goes beyond even the license assumed by Pope in the virulent ferocity of its personal attack on a woman. This may be explained, or at least illustrated, by the fact that Ben Jonson's views regarding womanhood in general were radically cynical though externally chivalrous : a charge which can be brought against no other poet or dramatist of his age. He could pay more splendid compliments than any of them to this or that particular woman ; the deathless epitaph on 'Sydney's sister, Pembroke's mother,' is but the crowning flower of a garland, the central jewel of a set ; but no man has said coarser (I had well-nigh written, viler) things against the sex to which these exceptionally honoured patronesses belonged. This characteristic is not more significant than the

corresponding evidence given by comparison of
his readiness to congratulate and commend other
poets and poeticules for work not always worthy
of his notice, and at the same time to indulge in
such sweeping denunciation of all contemporary
poetry as would not have misbecome the utterance
of incarnate envy—in other words, as might have
fallen from the lips of Byron.   See, for one most
flagrant and glaring example of what might seem
the very lunacy of malignity, a passage in what
Coleridge has justly called 'his splendid dedication
of *The Fox.*'   Here he talks of raising 'the
despised head of poetry again, *and stripping her
out of those rotten and base rags wherewith the
times have adulterated her form.*'   It is difficult to
resist a temptation to emulate Ben Jonson's own
utmost vehemence of language when we remember
that this sentence is dated the 11th of February,
1607.   Nine years before the death of Shakespeare
the greatest writer of all time, the most wonderful
human creature of all ages, was in the very zenith
of his powers and his glory.   And this was a
contemporary poet's view of the condition of contemporary poetry.   He was not more unlucky as
a courtier and a prophet when he proclaimed the
triumphant security of the English government

as twice ensured by the birth of the future King James II.

The memorial ode on the death of Sir Henry Morison has thoughtful and powerful touches in it, as well as one stanza so far above the rest that it gains by a process which would impair its effect if the poem were on the whole even a tolerably good one. The famous lines on ' the plant and flower of light' can be far better enjoyed when cut away from the context. The opening is as eccentrically execrable as the epode of the solitary strophe which redeems from all but unqualified execration a poem in which Gifford finds ' the very soul of Pindar '—whose reputation would in that case be the most inexplicable of riddles. Far purer in style and far more equable in metre is the ' ode gratulatory' to Lord Weston ; and the ' epithalamion' on the marriage of that nobleman's son, though not without inequalities, crudities, and platitudes, is on the whole a fine and dignified example of ceremonial poetry. Another of the laureate's best effusions of official verse is the short ode which bids his ' gentle Muse ' rouse herself to celebrate the king's birthday, ' though now our green conceits be grey,' with good wishes which have a tragic ring in the modern reader's ear.

more unequal poem than the elegy on the
Marchioness of Winchester is hardly to be found
anywhere ; but the finest passages are noble indeed.
The elegiac poems on the famous *demi-mondaine*
Venetia Stanley, who made a comparatively respectable end as Lady Digby, are equally startling and
amusing in their attribution to that heroine of a
character which would justify the beatification if
not the canonization of its immaculate possessor.
The first of these is chiefly remarkable for a
singular Scotticism—' where Seraphim *take tent* of
ordering all ' ; the fragment of the second, as an
early attempt—I know not whether it be the
earliest—to introduce the *terza rima* into English
verse.   There are one or two fine stanzas in the
fourth, and the *Apotheosis* of this singular saint has
a few good couplets ; it contains, however, probably
the most horrible and barbarous instance of inversion which the violated language can display :

> *in her hand*
> *With boughs of palm,* a crownèd victrice stand.

Such indefinable enormities as this cannot but
incline us to think that this great scholar, this
laurelled invader and conqueror of every field and
every province of classic learning, was *intus et in*

cute an irreclaimable and incurable barbarian. And assuredly this impression will be neither removed nor modified when we come to examine his translations from Latin poetry. If the report is to be believed which attributes to Ben Jonson the avowal of an opinion that above all things he excelled in translation, it must be admitted that for once the foolish theory which represents men of genius as incapable of recognizing what is or is not their best work or their most distinguishing faculty is justified and exemplified after a fashion so memorable that the exception must be invoked to prove the rule. For a worse translator than Ben Jonson never committed a double outrage on two languages at once. I should be reluctant to quote examples of this lamentable truth, if it were not necessary to vindicate his contemporaries from such an imputation as is conveyed in the general belief that his method of translation is merely the method of his age. The fact is that it is as exceptionally abominable as his genius, when working on its own proper and original lines, is exceptionally admirable. I am no great lover of Horace, but I cannot pretend to think that the words

Si torrere jecur quæris idoneum

are adequately rendered by the words

> If a fit liver thou dost seek to toast.

Fate and fire did a double injury, if not a double injustice, to Ben Jonson, when his commentary on Horace's *Art of Poetry* was consumed and his translation of the text preserved. The commentary in which Donne was represented under the name of Criticus must have been one of the most interesting and valuable of Jonson's prose works : the translation is one of those miracles of incompetence, incongruity, and insensibility, which must be seen to be believed. It may be admitted that there is a very happy instance of exact and pointed rendering from the ninth and tenth lines of the original in the eleventh and twelfth lines of the translation.

> Pictoribus atque poetis
> Quidlibet audendi semper fuit æqua potestas.
> Scimus.

Pope himself could not have rendered this well-known passage more neatly, more smoothly, more perfectly and more happily than thus—

> But equal power to painter and to poet
> Of daring all hath still been given : we know it.

And in the seventh line following we come upon this indescribable horror—an abomination of which

Abraham Fraunce or Gabriel Harvey would by charitable readers have been considered incapable : as perhaps indeed they were.

> A scarlet piece or two stitch'd in ; when or
> Diana's grove or altar, *with the bor-*
> *D'ring* circles of swift waters, &c , &c.

'The bellman writes better verses,' said Mr. Osbaldistone, when he threw poor Frank's away. Walt Whitman writes no worse, a modern critic will reflect on reading these.

The version of one of Martial's gracefullest epigrams flows more pleasantly than usual till it ends with a horrible jolt, thus :—

> He that but living half his days dies such,
> Makes his life longer than 'twas given him, much.

And Echo answers—Much! Gifford, however, waxes ecstatic over these eight lines. 'It is the most beautiful of all the versions of this elegant poem,' and, if we may believe him, 'clearly and fully expresses the whole of its meaning.' Witness the second line—

> Thou worthy in eternal flower to fare.

That is no more English than it is Latin—no more accurate than it is intelligible. The original is as simple as it is lovely :—

> Liber in æternâ vivere digne rosâ.

It would be worse than superfluous to look among his other versions from Horace for further evidence of Ben Jonson's incomparable incompetence as a translator. But as this has been hitherto very insufficiently insisted on,—his reputation as a poet and a scholar standing apparently between the evidence of this fact and the recognition of it,—I will give one crowning example from *The Poetaster.* This is what Virgil is represented as reading to Augustus—and Augustus as hearing without a shriek of agony and horror.

> Meanwhile the skies 'gan thunder, and in tail [1]
> Of that fell pouring storms of sleet and hail.

'In tail of that'! *Proh Deûm atque hominum fidem!* And it is Virgil—Virgil, of all men and all poets—to whom his traducer has the assurance to attribute this inexpressible atrocity of outrage!

The case of Ben Jonson is the great standing example of a truth which should never be forgotten or overlooked ; that no amount of learning, of labour, or of culture will supply the place of natural taste and native judgment—will avail in any slightest degree to confer the critical faculty upon a man to whom nature has denied it. Just judg-

---

[1] Compare *Æn.* iv. 160.

ment of others, just judgment of himself, was all
but impossible to this great writer, this consummate
and indefatigable scholar, this generous and enthusiastic friend.   The noble infirmity of excess in
benevolence is indisputably no less obvious in three
great writers of our own century ; great, each of
them, like Ben Jonson, in prose as well as in verse :
one of them greater than he, one of them equal,
and one of them hardly to be accounted equal with
him.   Victor Hugo, Walter Savage Landor, and
Théophile Gautier, were doubtless as exuberant
in generosity— the English poet was perhaps as
indiscriminate in enthusiasm of patronage or of
sympathy—as even the promiscuous panegyrist of
Shakespeare, of Fletcher, of Chapman, of Drayton,
of Browne, of Brome, and of May ; and moreover
of one Stephens, of one Rutter, of one Wright, of
one Warre, and of one Filmer.   Of these last five
names, that of the worthy Master Joseph Rutter—
Ben's ' dear son, and right learned friend '—is the
only one which signifies to me the existence of an
author not utterly unknown.   His spiritual father
or theatrical sponsor is most copious and most
cordial in his commendations of the good man's
pastoral drama ; he has not mentioned its one
crowning excellence— the quality for which, having

tried it every night for upwards of six weeks running, I can confidently and conscientiously recommend it.   Chloral is not only more dangerous but very much less certain as a soporific : the sleeplessness which could resist the influence of Mr. Rutter's verse can be curable only by dissolution ; the eyes which can keep open through the perusal of six consecutive pages must never hope to find rest but in the grave.

The many ceremonial or occasional poems addressed to friends and patrons of various ranks and characters, from the king and queen to a Mr. Burges and a Mr. Squib, are of equally various interest, now graver and now lighter, to a careful student of Ben Jonson as a poet and a man.   Nor, when due account is taken of the time and its conventional habits of speech, does it seem to me that any of them can be justly charged with servility or flattery, or, as the writer might have said, with 'assentation.'   But these effusions or improvisations are of no more serious importance than the *Leges* exquisitely neat and terse composition of *Convivales* the ' Leges Convivales,' or the admirable good sense and industry, the admirable perspicacity and perspicuity, which will be recognized no less in the Latin than in the English part of his

English Grammar. It is interesting to observe an anticipation of Landor's principle with respect to questions of orthography, in the preference English Grammar. given to the Latin form of spelling for words of Latin derivation, while admitting that this increase of accuracy would bring the written word no nearer to the sound uttered in speaking. The passage is worth transcription as an example of delicately scrupulous accuracy and subtly conscientious refinement in explanation.

Alii hæc haud inconsultò scribunt *abil, stabil, fabul*; tanquam a fontibus *habilis, stabilis, fabula* : veriùs, sed nequicquam proficiunt Nam consideratiùs auscultanti nec *i* nec *u* est, sed tinnitus quidam, *vocalis* naturam habens, quæ naturaliter his liquidis inest.

A point on which I am sorry to rest uncertain whether Landor would have felt as much sympathy with Jonson's view as I feel myself is the regret expressed by the elder poet for the loss of the Saxon characters that distinguished the two different sounds now both alike expressed, and expressed with equal inaccuracy, by the two letters *th*. ' And in this,' says Jonson—as it seems to me, most reasonably, ' consists the greatest difficulty of our alphabet and true writing.'

The text of the grammar, both Latin and

English, requires careful revision and correction; but indeed as much must be said of the text of Jonson's works in general. Gifford did very much for it, but he left not a little to be done. And the arrangement adopted in Colonel Cunningham's beautiful and serviceable edition of 1875 is the most extraordinary—at least, I hope and believe so—on record. All the misreadings of the edition of 1816 are retained in the text, where they stand not merely uncorrected but unremarked; so that the bewildered student must refer at random, on the even chance of disappointment, to an appendix in which he may find them irregularly registered, with some occasional comment on the previous editor's negligence and caprice: a method, to put it as mildly as possible, somewhat provocative of strong language on the part of a studious and belated reader—language for which it cannot rationally be imagined that it is he who will be registered by the recording angel as culpably responsible. What is wanted in the case of so great an English classic is of course nothing less than this: a careful and complete edition of all his extant writings, with all the various readings of the various editions published during his lifetime. This is the very least that should be exacted; and this is less than has yet been supplied. Edition after edition of Shakespeare is put forth under the auspices of scholars or of dunces without a full and plain enumeration of the exact differences of text —the corrections, suppressions, alterations, and modifications—which distinguish the text of the quartos from the too frequently garbled and mangled, the sometimes transfigured and glorified text of the folio. And consequently not one devoted student in a thousand has a chance of knowing what he has a right to know of the gradations and variations in expression, the development and the self-discipline in display, of the most transcendent intelligence that ever illuminated humanity. And in the case of Shakespeare's most loyal comrade and panegyrist—though sometimes, it may be, his rather captious rival and critic—the neglect of his professed devotees and editorial interpreters has been scarcely less scandalous and altogether as incomprehensible. In every edition which makes any pretence to completeness, or to satisfaction of a serious student's indispensable requisites and inevitable demands, the first text of *Every Man in his Humour* should of course be given in full. Snatches and scraps of it are given in the notes to the edition of 1816; the first act is reprinted—the first act alone—in the appendix to the first volume of the edition of 1875. What would be said by Hellenists or Latinists if such contemptuous indolence, such insolence of neglect, were displayed by the editor of a Greek or Latin poet—assuming that his edition had been meant for other than fourth-form or fifth-form service? Compare the devotion of their very best editors to Shakespeare and to Jonson with the devotion of Mr. Ellis to Catullus and Mr. Munro to Lucretius. It is a shame that Englishmen should not be forthcoming who would think it worth while to expend as much labour, and would be competent to bring that labour to as good an end, in the service of their own immortal countrymen, as is expended and as is attained by classical scholars in the service of alien and not more adorable gods. And on one point—a point indeed of more significance than importance—the capricious impertinence of such editors as do condescend to undertake any part of such a task is so inexplicable except on one supposition that we are tempted to embrace, or at least to accept, the assumption that the editor (for instance) of Ben Jonson considers the author of *The Silent Woman, Bartholomew Fair*, and certain metrical emetics classified under the head of *Epigrams*, as a writer fit to be placed in the hands of schoolgirls. And even then it is difficult to imagine why we come upon certain rows of asterisks in the record of his conversations with Drummond, and in the anonymous interlude written —as Gifford supposes —' for the christening of a son of the Earl of Newcastle, to whom the king or the prince stood godfather.' Even if Jonson had taken—as on such an occasion it would be strange if he had taken—the utmost license of his friends Aristophanes and Rabelais, this would be no reason for treating the reader like a schoolboy or a Dauphin. What a man of genius has written for a public occasion is public property thenceforward and for ever : and the pretence of a man like Gifford to draw the line and determine the limit of publicity is inexpressibly preposterous.

The little interlude, however broad and even coarse in its realistic pleasantry, is a quaint and spirited piece of work ; but there are other matters in Colonel Cunningham's appendix which have no right, demonstrable or imaginable, to the place they occupy. It is incredible, it is inconceivable, that Jonson should ever have written such a line as this by way of a Latin verse :

Macte : tuo scriptores lectoresque labore (!!!)

' Les chassepots partiraient d'eux-mêmes '—birch would make itself into spontaneous rods for the schoolboy who could perpetrate so horrible an atrocity. The repulsive and ridiculous rubbish which has ignorantly and absurdly been taken for 'a fragment of one of the lost quaternions of *Eupheme*' is part, I am sorry to say, of an elegy by Francis Beaumont on one Lady Markham. It is an intolerable scandal that the public should be content to endure such an outrage as the intrusion of another man's abominable absurdities into the text of such a writer as Ben Jonson. This effusion of his young friend's, which must surely have been meant as a joke—and a very bad, not to say a very brutal one, is probably the most hideous nonsense ever written on the desecrated subject of death and decay. A smaller but a serious example of negligence and incompetence is patent in the text of the ten lines contributed by Jonson to the *Annalia Dubrensia*—that most pleasant and curious athletic anthology, the reissue of which is one of the wellnigh countless obligations conferred on students of the period by the devoted industry, energy, and ability of Dr. Grosart. He, of course, could not fail to see that the first of these lines was corrupt. ' I cannot bring my *Muse* to dropp

Vies' is obviously neither sense nor metre. It is rather with diffidence than with confidence that I would suggest the reading *double* in place of the palpably corrupt word *drop*: but from Gifford's explanation of the gambling term *vie* I should infer that this reading, which certainly rectifies the metre, might also restore the sense. Another obvious error is to be noted in the doggrel lines on Lady Ogle, which afford a curious and compact example of Ben Jonson's very worst vices of style and metre. Still, as Ben was not in the habit of writing flat nonsense, we ought evidently to read 'in the *sight* of Angels,' not, as absurdly printed in the edition of 1875 (ix. 326), 'in the Light'; especially as the next verse ends with that word. The commendatory verses on *Cynthia's Revenge* which reappear at page 346 of the same volume had appeared on page 332 of the volume immediately preceding. Such editorial derelictions and delinquencies are enough to inoculate the most patient reader's humour with the acerbity of Gifford's or Carlyle's. Again, this appendix gives only one or two fragments of the famous additional scenes to *The Spanish Tragedy*, while the finest and most important passages are omitted and ignored. For one thing, however, we have reason to be grateful to the compiler who has inserted for the first time among Ben Jonson's works the fine and flowing stanzas described by their author as an allegoric ode. This poem, which in form is Horatian, has no single stanza so beautiful or so noble as the famous third strophe of the Pindaric ode to Sir Lucius Cary on the death of Sir Henry Morison ; but its general superiority in purity of style and fluidity of metre is as remarkable as the choice and use of proper names with such a dexterous felicity as to emulate while it recalls the majestic and magnificent instincts of Marlowe and of Milton.

If the fame of Ben Jonson were in any degree dependent on his minor or miscellaneous works in verse, it would be difficult to assign him a place above the third or fourth rank of writers belonging to the age of Shakespeare. His station in the first class of such writers, and therefore in the front rank of English authors, is secured mainly by the excellence of his four masterpieces in comedy ; *The Fox* and *The Alchemist, The Staple of News* and *Every Man in his Humour* : but a single leaf of his *Discoveries* is worth all his lyrics, tragedies, elegies, and epigrams together. That golden little book of noble thoughts and subtle observations is

the one only province of his vast and varied
empire which yet remains for us to examine ; and
in none other will there be found more ample and
more memorable evidence how truly great a man
demands our homage—'on this side idolatry'—
for the imperishable memory of Ben Jonson.

III. DISCOVERIES

III

DISCOVERIES

THAT chance is the ruler of the world I should be sorry to believe and reluctant to affirm; but it would be difficult for any competent and careful student to maintain that chance is not the ruler of the world of letters. Gray's odes are still, I suppose, familiar to thousands who know nothing of Donne's *Anniversaries*; and Bacon's Essays are conventionally if not actually familiar to thousands who know nothing of Ben Jonson's *Discoveries*. And yet it is certain that in fervour of inspiration, in depth and force and glow of thought and emotion and expression, Donne's verses are as far above Gray's as Jonson's notes or observations on men and morals, on principles and on facts, are superior to Bacon's in truth of insight, in breadth of view, in vigour of reflection and in concision of eloquence. The dry curt style of the statesman, docked and trimmed into sentences that are

regularly snapped off or snipped down at the
close of each deliverance, is as alien and as far
from the fresh and vigorous spontaneity of the
poet's as is the trimming and hedging morality of
the essay on 'simulation and dissimulation' from
the spirit and instinct of the man who 'of all
things loved to be called honest.' But indeed,
from the ethical point of view which looks merely
or mainly to character, the comparison is little less
than an insult to the Laureate; and from the
purely intelligent or æsthetic point of view I
should be disposed to say, or at least inclined to
think, that the comparison would be hardly less
unduly complimentary to the Chancellor.

For at the very opening of these *Explorata, or
Discoveries*, we find ourselves in so high and so
pure an atmosphere of feeling and of thought that
we cannot but recognize and rejoice in the presence and the influence of one of the noblest,
manliest, most honest and most helpful natures
that ever dignified and glorified a powerful intelligence and an admirable genius. In the very first
note, the condensed or concentrated quintessence
of a Baconian essay on Fortune, we find these
among other lofty and weighty words: Heaven
prepares good men with crosses; but no ill can

happen to a good man.' 'That which happens to any man, may to every man. But it is in his reason what he accounts it and will make it.'

There is perhaps in the structure of this sentence something too much of the Latinist— too strong a flavour of the style of Tacitus in its elaborate if not laborious terseness of expression. But the following could hardly be bettered.

No man is so foolish but may give another good counsel sometimes ; and no man is so wise but may easily err, if he will take no other's counsel but his own. But very few men are wise by their own counsel, or learned by their own teaching. For he that was only taught by himself had a fool to his master.

The mind's ear may find or fancy a silvery ring of serene good sense in the note of that reflection ; but the ring of what follows is pure gold.

There is a necessity all men should love their country ; he that professeth the contrary may be delighted with his words, but his heart is [not] there.

The magnificent expansion or paraphrase of this noble thought in the fourth scene of Landor's magnificent tragedy of *Count Julian* should be familiar to all capable students of English poetry at its purest and proudest height of sublime con-templation. That probably or rather undoubtedly unconscious echo of the sentiment of an older poet and patriot has in it the prolonged reverberation and repercussion of music which we hear in the echoes of thunder or a breaking sea.

Again, how happy in the bitterness of its truth is the next remark : ' Natures that are hardened to evil you shall sooner break than make straight : they are like poles that are crooked and dry : there is no attempting them.' And how grand is this :

I cannot think nature is so spent and decayed that she can bring forth nothing worth her former years. She is always the same, like herself ; and when she collects her strength,[1] is abler still. *Men are decayed, and studies : she is not.*

Jonson never wrote a finer verse than that ; and very probably he never observed that it was a verse.

The next note is one of special interest to all students of the great writer who has so often been described as a blind worshipper and a servile disciple of classical antiquity.

' I know nothing can conduce more to letters,' says the too obsequious observer of Tacitus and of Cicero in

---

[1] As in the production of Shakespeare—if his good friend Ben had but known it.

the composition of his Roman tragedies, 'than to examine the writings of the ancients, and not to rest on their sole authority, or take all upon trust from them; provided the plagues of judging and pronouncing against them be away; such as are envy, bitterness, precipitation, impudence, and scurril scoffing. For, to all the observations of the ancients, we have our own experience; which if we will use and apply, we have better means to pronounce. It is true they opened the gates, and made the way, that went before us; but as guides, not commanders: *Non domini nostri sed duces fuere.* Truth lies open to all; it is no man's several. *Patet omnibus veritas: nondum est occupata. Multum ex illâ etiam futuris relictum est.'*[1]

Time and space would fail me to transcribe all that is worth transcription, to comment on everything that deserves commentary, in this treasure-house of art and wisdom, eloquence and good sense. But the following extract could be passed over by no eye but a mole's or a bat's.

I do not desire to be equal with those that went before; but to have my reason examined with theirs, and so much faith to be given them, or me, as those shall evict [in modern English—if the text is not corrupt—'as the comparison or confrontation of theirs with mine shall elicit']. I am neither author nor fautor of any sect. I will have no man addict himself to me; but if I have

---

[1] The scandalously neglected text reads *relicta.* Perhaps we should read ' Multa—relicta sunt.'

anything right, defend it as Truth's, not mine, save as it conduceth to a common good. It profits not me to have any man fence or fight for me, to flourish, or take my side. Stand for Truth, and 'tis enough.

The haughty vindication of 'arts that respect the mind' as 'nobler than those that serve the body, though we less can be without them' (the latter), is at once amusingly and admirably Jonsonian. Admitting the ignoble fact that without such 'arts' as 'tillage, spinning, weaving, building, &c.,' 'we could scarce sustain life a day,' a proposition which it certainly would seem difficult to dispute, he proceeds in the loftiest tone of professional philosophy : ' But these were the works of every hand ; the other of the brain only, and those the most generous and exalted wits and spirits, that cannot rest or acquiesce. The mind of man is still fed with labour : *opere pascitur.*'

This conscientious and self-conscious pride of intellect finds even a nobler and more memorable expression in the admirable words which instruct or which remind us of the truth that 'it is as great a spite to be praised in the wrong place, and by the wrong person, as can be done to a noble nature.' A sentence worthy to be set beside the fittest motto for all loyal men—' Æqua laus est a laudatis laudari et ab improbis improbari.' Which it would be well that every man worthy to apply it should lay to heart, and act and bear himself accordingly.

It is to be wished that the dramatist and humourist had always or had usually borne in mind the following excellent definition or reflection of the aphoristic philosopher or student : 'A tedious person is one a man would leap a steeple from, gallop down any steep hill to avoid him ; forsake his meat, sleep, nature itself, with all her benefits, to shun him.' What then shall we say of the courtiers in *Cynthia's Revels* and the vapourers in *Bartholomew Fair* ?

The following is somewhat especially suggestive of a present political application ; and would find its appropriate setting in a modern version of the *Irish Masque*.

He is a narrow-minded man that affects a triumph in any glorious study ; but to triumph in a lie, and a lie themselves have forged, is frontless. Folly often goes beyond her bounds ; but Impudence knows none.

From the forty-third to the forty-eighth entry inclusive these disconnected notes should be read as a short continuous essay on envy and calumny.

For weight, point, and vigour, it would hardly be possible to overpraise it.

In the admirable note on such 'foolish lovers' as 'wish the same to their friends as their enemies would,' merely that they might have occasion to display the constancy of their regard, there is a palpable and preposterous misprint, which reduces to nonsense a remarkably fine passage : 'They make a causeway to their courtesy by injury ; as if it were not honester to do nothing than to seek a way to do good by a mischief.' For the obviously right word ' courtesy' the unspeakable editors read ' country ' ; which let him explain who can.

The two notes on injuries and benefits are observable for their wholesome admixture of common sense with magnanimity.

Injuries do not extinguish courtesies : they only suffer them not to appear fair. For a man that doth me an injury after a courtesy takes not away that courtesy, but defaces it : as he that writes other verses upon my verses takes not away the first letters, but hides them.

Surely no sentence more high-minded and generous than that was ever written : nor one more sensible and dignified than this :—

The doing of courtesies aright is the mixing of the

respects for his own sake and for mine. He that doeth them merely for his own sake is like one that feeds his cattle to sell them: he hath his horse well drest for Smithfield.

The following touch of mental autobiography is not less interesting than curious. Had Shakespeare but left us the like!

I myself could in my youth have repeated all that ever I had made, and so continued till I was past forty: since, it is much decayed in me. Yet I can repeat whole books that I have read, and poems of some selected friends, which I have liked to charge my memory with. It was wont to be faithful to me; but, shaken with age now, and sloth, which weakens the strongest abilities, it may perform somewhat, but cannot promise much. By exercise it is to be made better, and serviceable. Whatsoever I pawned with it while I was young, and a boy, it offers me readily, and without stops: but what I trust to it now, or have done of later years, it lays up more negligently, and oftentimes loses; so that I receive mine own (though frequently called for) as if it were new and bor- -rowed. Nor do I always find presently from it what I seek: but while I am doing another thing, that I laboured for will come; and what I sought with trouble will offer itself when I am quiet. Now in some men [was Shakespeare, we must ask ourselves, one of these?] I have found it as happy as nature, who, whatsoever they read or pen, they can say without book presently; as if they did then write in their mind. And it is more a wonder in such as have a swift style, for their memories are commonly slowest; such as torture their writings, and go into council for every word, must needs fix somewhat, and make it their own at last, though but through their own vexation.

I cannot but imagine that Jonson must have witnessed this wonder in the crowning case of Shakespeare; the swiftness of whose 'style' or composition was matter of general note.

The anti-Gallican or anti-democratic view of politics can never be more vividly or happily presented thàn in these brilliant and incisive words :—

Suffrages in Parliament are numbered, not weighed: nor can it be otherwise in those public councils, *where nothing is so unequal as the equality* : for there, how odd soever men's brains or wisdoms are, their power is always even and the same.

But the most cordial hater or scorner of parliaments, whether from the Carlylesque or the Bonapartist point of vantage, must allow that the truth expressed in the two first sentences following is more certain and more precious than the doctrine just cited.

Truth is man's proper good, and the only immortal thing was given to our mortality to use. No good

Christian or ethnic, if he be honest, can miss it: no statesman or patriot should. For without truth all the actions of mankind are craft, malice, or what you will rather than wisdom. Homer says he hates him worse than hell-mouth that utters one thing with his tongue and keeps another in his breast. Which high expression was grounded on divine reason: for a lying mouth is a stinking pit, and murders with the contagion it venteth. Besides, nothing is lasting that is feigned; it will have another face than it had ere long. As Euripides saith, 'No lie ever grows old.'

It would be well if this were so: but the inveterate reputation of Euripides as a dramatic poet is hardly reconcilable with the truth of his glibly optimistic assumption. Nor, had that fluent and facile dealer in flaccid verse and sentimental sophistry spoken truth for once in this instance, should we have had occasion to wonder at the admiration expressed for him by the most subtle and sincere, the most profound and piercing intelligence of our time; nor could that sense of reverential amazement have found spontaneous expression in the following couplet of Hudibrastic doggrel :—

> That the huckster of pathos, whose gift was insipid ease,
> Finds favour with Browning, must puzzle Euripides.

But Jonson himself, it seems to me, was far

less trustworthy as a critic of poetry than as a judge on ethics or a student of character. The tone of supercilious goodwill and friendly condonation which distinguishes his famous note on Shakespeare is unmistakable except by the most wilful perversity of prepossession. His noble metrical tribute to Shakespeare's memory must of course be taken into account when we are disposed to think too hardly of this honest if egotistic eccentricity of error: but it would be foolish to suppose that the most eloquent cordiality of a ceremonial poem could express more of one man's real and critical estimate of another than a deliberate reflection of later date. And it needs the utmost possible exertion of charity, the most generous exercise of justice, to forgive the final phrase of preposterous patronage and considerate condescension—'There was ever more in him to be praised than to be pardoned.' The candid author of *Sejanus* could on the whole afford to admit so much with respect to the popular author of *Hamlet*.

In the subsequent essay, divided under ten several heads into ten several notes, on 'the difference of wits,' or the diversity of accomplishments and understandings, there is much worth

study for its soundness of judgment, its accuracy
of definition, and its felicity of expression. It
would be well if educational and professional for-
malists would bear in mind the truth that 'there
is no doctrine will do good, where nature is wanting'; and nothing could be neater, terser, or truer
than the definition of those characters 'that are
forward and bold; and these will do every little
thing easily; I mean, that is hard by and next
them, which they will utter unretarded without
any shamefastness. These never perform much,
but quickly. They are what they are, on the
sudden; they show presently, like grain that,
scattered on the top of the ground, shoots up, but
takes no root; has a yellow blade, but the ear
empty. They are wits of good promise at first,
but there is an ingenîstitium—a wit-stand: they
stand still at sixteen, they get no higher.'

As well worth remark and recollection are the
succeeding notes on 'others, that labour only to
ostentation; and are ever more busy about the
colours and surface of a work than in the matter
and foundation: for that is hid, the other is seen';
and on those whose style of composition is pur-
posely 'rough and broken—and if it would come
gently, they trouble it of purpose. They would

not have it run without rubs : as if that style were more strong and manly that struck the ear with a kind of unevenness. These men err not by chance, but knowingly and willingly ; they are like men that affect a fashion by themselves, have some singularity in a ruff, cloak, or hat-band ; or their beards specially cut to provoke beholders, and set a mark upon themselves. They would be reprehended, while they are looked on. And this vice, one, that is in authority with the rest, loving, delivers over to them to be imitated ; so that oft-times the faults which he fell into, the others seek for : this is the danger, when vice becomes a pre-cedent.'

It is difficult to imagine that Jonson was not here thinking of the great writer whom 'he es-teemed the first poet in the world in some things,' but upon whom he passed the too sweeping though too plausible sentence 'that Donne, for not being understood, would perish.' Nor can we suppose that he was not alluding to Daniel—the inoffensive object of his implacable satire—when he laid a 'chastising hand' on 'others that have no composition at all, but a kind of tuning and rhyming fall, in what they write. It runs and slides, and only makes a sound. Women's poets

they are called, as you have women's tailors.—
You may sound these wits and find the depth of
them with your middle finger. They are cream-
bowl- (or but puddle-) deep.'

An amusing anticipation of the peculiar genius
for ĕlaborate mendacity which distinguishes and
connects the names of De Quincey and Mérimée
will be found in Jonson's words of stern and indig-
nant censure on ' some who, after they have got
authority, or, which is less, opinion, by their
writings, to have read much, dare presently to feign
whole books and authors, and lie safely. For what
never was will not easily be found ; not by the
most curious.' Certainly it was not by the innocent
readers whose research into the original authorities
for the history of the revolt of the Tartars, or
whose interest in the original text of Clara
Gazul's plays and the Illyrian ballads of *La
Guzla*, must have given such keen delight to
those two frontless and matchless charlatans of
genius.

The keen and scornful intelligence of Jonson
finds no less admirable expression in the two
succeeding notes ; of which the first sets a brand
on such cunning plagiarists as protest against all
reading, and so ' think to divert the sagacity of

their readers from themselves, and cool the scent of
their own fox-like thefts ; ' but, as he proceeds to
observe, ' the obstinate contemners of all helps and
arts are in a ' wretcheder ' case than even these.
His description of such pretenders is too lifelike,
and too vivid in its perennial veracity, to be overlooked ; ' such as presuming on their own naturals
(which perhaps are excellent) dare deride all dili-
gence, and seem to mock at the terms when they
understand not the things ; thinking that way to
get off wittily with their ignorance. These are
imitated often by such as are their peers in negligence, though they cannot be in nature ; and they
utter all they can think with a kind of violence and
indisposition ; unexamined, without relation to
person, place, or any fitness else ; and the more
wilful and stubborn they are in it, the more learned
they are esteemed of the multitude, through their
excellent vice of judgment ; who think those things
the stronger, that have no art ; as if to break were
better than to open ; or to rend asunder, gentler
than to loose.'

In the tenth section or subdivision of this
irregular and desultory but incisive and masterly
essay we find a singular combination of critical
insight with personal prejudice—of general truth

with particular error. But the better part is excellent alike in reflection and in expression.

It cannot but come to pass that these men who commonly seek to do more than enough may sometimes happen on something that is good and great; but very seldom: and when it comes it doth not recompense the rest of their ill.—The true artificer will not run away from nature, as he were afraid of her; or depart from life, and the likeness of truth; but speak to the capacity of his hearers.

The rest of the note is valuable as a studious and elaborate expression of Jonson's theory or ideal of dramatic poetry, couched in apt and eloquent phrases of thoughtful and balanced rhetoric; regrettable only for the insulting reference to the first work of a yet greater poet than himself, to whose 'mighty line' he had paid immortal homage in an earlier and a better mood of judgment.

But however prone he may be to error or perversity in particular instances or in personal examples, he is constantly and nobly right in his axiomatic reflections and his general observations. The following passage seems to me a magnificent illustration of this truth.

I know no disease of the soul but ignorance; not of

the arts and sciences, but of itself: yet relating to those it is a pernicious evil, the darkener of man's life, the disturber of his reason, and the common confounder of truth; with which a man goes groping in the dark, no otherwise than if he were blind. Great understandings are most racked and troubled with it; nay, sometimes they will rather choose to die than not to know the things they study for.[1] Think then what an evil it is, and what [a] good the contrary.

The ensuing note on knowledge has less depth of direct insight, less force of practical reason; but the definition which follows is singularly eloquent and refined, however scholastic and irrational in its casuistic and rhetorical subtlety.

Knowledge is the action of the soul, and is perfect without the senses,[2] as having the seeds of all science and virtue in itself; but not without the service of the senses; by these organs the soul works: she is a perpetual agent, prompt and subtle; but often flexible and erring, entangling herself like a silkworm: but her reason is a weapon with two edges, and cuts through.

I am inclined to suspect that we may discern in

[1] No modern reader of these lofty words can fail to call to mind the sublime pathos and the historic interest of Mr. Browning's glorious poem, *A Grammarian's Funeral*.

[2] It is a pity we are not told how; for to the ordinary intelligence of reasoning mankind it would appear that 'without the senses' not only could knowledge not be perfect, but it could not even exist in the most inchoate or embryonic phase of being.

the next note another fragment of autobiography. For it may be doubted whether 'the boon Delphic god,' so admirably described by his faithful acolyte Marmion as presiding in the form of a human Laureate over the Bacchanalian oracle of Apollo, can ever have been able to say with equal truth of another than himself,

I have known a man vehement on both sides, that knew no mean either to intermit his studies or call upon them again. When he hath set himself to writing, he would join night to day, press upon himself without release, not minding it, till he fainted; and when he got off, resolve himself into all sports and looseness again, that it was almost a despair to draw him to his book; but once got to it, he grew stronger and more earnest by the ease. His whole powers were renewed: he would work out of himself what he desired; but with such excess, as his study could not be ruled: he knew not how to dispose his own abilities or husband them, he was of that immoderate power against himself. Nor was he only a strong but an absolute speaker and writer; but his subtlety did not show itself; his judgment thought that a vice: for the ambush hurts more that is hid. He never forced his language, nor went out of the highway of speaking, but for some great necessity, or apparent profit: for he denied figures to be invented for ornament, but for aid: and still thought it an extreme madness to bend or wrest that which ought to be right.

If any reader should think such a mixture of
critical self-examination and complacent self-glori-
fication impossible to any man of indisputable
genius and of general good sense, that reader is
not yet ' sealed of the tribe of Ben ' ; he has not
arrived at a due appreciation of the writer's general
strength and particular weakness as a critic and a
workman, an artist and a thinker.

The note on famous orators is remarkable for its
keen discrimination and appreciation of various
talents ; and the subsequent analysis or definition
of Bacon's great gifts as a speaker, which has been
often enough quoted to dispense with any fresh
citation, is only less fine than the magnificent
tribute paid a little further on to the same great
man in his days of adversity. It may well be
questioned whether there exists a finer example
of English prose than the latter famous passage ;
where sublimity is resolved into pathos, and pathos
dilates into sublimity.   His idealism of monarchy,
however irrational it may seem to us, has a finer
side to it than belongs to the blind superstition of
such a royalist as Fletcher. Witness this striking
and touching interpretation of an old metaphor :
' Why are prayers said with Orpheus to be the
daughters of Jupiter, but that princes are thereby

admonished that the petitions of the wretched
ought to have more weight with them than the
laws themselves?' And the following note gives a
better and a kindlier impression of King James I.
than anything else—as far as I know—recorded
of that singular sovereign.

It was a great accumulation to his majesty's deserved
praise, that men might openly visit and pity those whom
his greatest prisons had at any time received, or his laws
condemned.

The note on 'the attribute of a prince' is rather
Baconian than Jonsonian in its cult of 'prudence'
as 'his chief art and safety'; but the peculiar and
practical humour of Jonson's observant and studious
satire is well exemplified in his strictures on such
theological controversialists as 'are like swaggerers
in a tavern, that catch that which stands next
them, the candlesticks or pots—turn everything
into a weapon: ofttimes they fight blindfold, and
both beat the air. The one milks a he-goat, the
other holds under a sieve. Their arguments are as
fluxive as liquor spilt upon a table, which with
your finger you may drain as you will.' But the
remarks on 'untimely boasting' are especially
worth transcription, both for their own real excellence and for the unconscious but inexpressible

drollery of such an utterance from the 'capacious mouth' which had so often and so loudly set forth under divers names and figures the claims and the merits of Ben Jonson.

Men that talk of their own benefits are not believed to talk of them because they have done them, but to have done them because they might talk of them. That which had been great if another had reported it of them vanisheth and is nothing if he that did it speak of it. For men when they cannot destroy the deed, will yet be glad to take advantage of the boasting and lessen it.

We may hope that these wise and weighty words were not written without some regretful if not repentant reminiscence of sundry occasions on which this rule of conduct had been grossly and grievously transgressed by the writer, to his own inevitable damage and discomfiture.

The note on flattery and flatterers is as exalted in its austerity as trenchant in its scorn. And the following remark 'on human life' is the condensed or distilled essence of a noble satire or a powerful essay.

I have considered our whole life is like a play, wherein every man, forgetful of himself, is in travail with expression of another. Nay, we so insist in imitating others, as we cannot (when it is necessary) return to ourselves;

like children that imitate the vices of stammerers so long, till at last they become such; and make the habit to another nature, as it is never forgotten.

There is a noble enthusiasm for goodness in the phrase which avers that 'good men are the stars, the planets of the ages wherein they live, and illustrate the times.' After an enumeration of scriptural instances, the poet adds this commentary : ' These, sensual men thought mad, because they would not be partakers or practisers of their madness. But they, placed high on the top of all virtue, looked down on the stage of the world, and contemned the play of fortune. For though the most be players, some must be spectators.'

And there is a fine touch of grave and bitter humour in the discovery ' that a feigned familiarity in great ones is a note of certain usurpation on the less. For great and popular men feign themselves to be servants to others, to make those slaves to them. So the fisher provides bait for the trout, roach, dace, &c., that they may be food to him.'

But finer by far and far more memorable than this is the following commentary on the fact that the emperor whose ' voice was worthier a headsman than a head, when he wished the people of Rome had but one neck,' 'found (when he fell) they had many hands.'

A tyrant, how great and mighty soever he may seem to cowards and sluggards, is but one creature, one animal.

That sentence is worthy of Landor ; and those who would reproach Ben Jonson with the extravagance of his monarchical doctrines or theories must admit that such royalism as is compatible with undisguised approval of regicide or tyrannicide might not irrationally be condoned by the sternest and most rigid of republicans.

The next eight notes or entries deal in a somewhat desultory fashion with the subject of government ; and display, as might be expected, a very singular combination or confusion of obsolete sophistry and superstition with rational and liberal intelligence. He attacks Machiavelli repeatedly, but there is a distinct streak of what is usually understood as Machiavellism in the remark, for example, that when a prince governs his people 'so as they have still need of his administration (for that is his art) he shall ever make and hold them faithful.' In answer to Machiavelli's principle of cruelty by proxy, he pleads with great and simple force of eloquence against all principles of cruelty whatever. Many noble passages might be quoted from this pleading ; but only a few can here be selected from the third and fourth, the sixth and seventh, of the entries above mentioned ; which may on the whole be considered, when all due reservation is made with regard to the monarchical principle or superstition, as composing altogether a concise and masterly essay on the art and the principles of wise and righteous government.

Many punishments sometimes and in some cases as much discredit a prince as many funerals a physician. The state of things is secured by clemency : severity represseth a few, but irritates more. The lopping of trees makes the boughs shoot out thicker ; and the taking away of some kind of enemies increaseth the number. It is then most gracious in a prince to pardon, when many about him would make him cruel ; to think then how much he can save, when others tell him how much he can destroy ; not to consider what the impotence of others hath demolished, but what his own greatness can sustain. These are a prince's virtues : and they that give him other counsels are but the hangman's factors.

But princes, by hearkening to cruel counsels, become in time obnoxious to the authors, their flatterers and ministers ; and are brought to that, that when they would they dare not change them ; they must go on, and defend cruelty with cruelty ; they cannot alter the habit. It is then grown necessary they must be as ill as those have made them : and in the end they will grow more hateful to themselves than to their subjects. Whereas, on the contrary, the merciful prince is safe in love, not in fear. He needs no emissaries, spies, intelligencers, to entrap true subjects. He fears no libels, no treasons. His people speak what they think, and talk openly what they do in secret. They have nothing in their breasts that they need a cipher for. He is guarded with his own benefits.

There is nothing with some princes sacred above their majesty ; or profane, but what violates their sceptres. But a prince with such a council [qu. counsel ?] is like the god Terminus of stone, his own landmark ; or (as it is in the fable) a crowned lion. . . . No men hate an evil prince more than they that helped to make him such. And none more boastingly weep his ruin than they that procured and practised it. The same path leads to ruin which did to rule, when men profess a license in government. A good king is a public servant.

A prince without letters is a pilot without eyes. All his government is groping. In sovereignty it is a most happy thing not to be compelled ; but so it is the most miserable not to be counselled. And how can he be counselled that cannot see to read the best counsellors, which are books ; for they neither flatter us nor hide from us ? He may hear, you will say ; but how shall he always be sure to hear truth ? or be counselled the best things, not the sweetest ? They say princes learn no art truly but the art of horsemanship. The reason is, the brave beast is no flatterer.   He will throw a prince as soon as his groom.   Which is an argument that the good counsellors to princes are the best instruments of a good age. For though the prince himself be of most prompt inclination to all virtue, yet the best pilots have need of mariners, besides sails, anchor, and other tackle.

It must be admitted that the royalism of this laureate is sufficiently tempered and allayed with rational or republican good sense to excite in the reader's mind a certain curiosity of conjecture as to the effect which might or which must have been produced on his royal patrons by the publication of opinions so irreconcilable with the tragically comic form of idolatry embodied in the heroes and expressed in the rhapsodies of Beaumont and Fletcher.   Amintor and Aëcius, Archas and Aubrey, are figures or types of unnatural heroism or preposterous devotion which are obviously and essentially wellnigh as far from Jonson's ideal of manhood and of duty as from Shakespeare's.

There is a quaint fierce touch of humour in the reflection that ' he which is sole heir to many rich men, having (beside his father's and uncle's) the estates of divers his kindred come to him by accession, must needs be richer than father or grandfather : so they which are left heirs *ex asse* ' (sole heirs) 'of all their ancestor's vices, and by their good husbandry improve the old, and daily purchase new, must needs be wealthier in vice, and have a greater revenue or stock of ill to spend on.' But this is only one in a score of instances which might be quoted to show that if a great English poet and humourist had left nothing behind him but this little book of 'maxims,' as the French call them—notes, observations, or reflections cast in a form more familiar to French than to English writers—he would still hold a place beside or above La Rochefoucauld, and beside if not above Chamfort. And yet, even among his countrymen, it may be feared that the sardonic wit and the cynical wisdom of the brilliant French patrician and the splendid French plebeian are familiar to many who have never cared to investigate the *Discoveries* of Ben Jonson.

Again we meet the strangely outspoken satirist and malcontent in the person of the court laureate who allowed himself to remark that 'the great thieves of a state are lightly' [usually or naturally] 'the officers of the crown: they hang the less still, play the pikes in the pond, eat whom they list. The net was never spread for the hawk or buzzard that hurt us, but the harmless birds ; they are good

meat.' But the critic of state consoles himself with
a reflection on the precarious tenure of their powers
enjoyed by such tenants or delegates of tyranny,
and cites against them a well-known witticism of
that great practical humourist King Louis XI.

The partially autobiographic or personal note
which follows this opens and closes at once nobly
and simply.

A good man will avoid the spot of any sin. The very
aspersion is grievous ; which makes him choose his way
in his life, as he would in his journey. The ill man rides
through all confidently ; he is coated and booted for it.
The oftener he offends, the more openly ; and the fouler,
the fitter in fashion. His modesty, like a riding-coat, the
more it is worn, is the less cared for. It is good enough
for the dirt still, and the ways he travels on.

No one will be surprised to find that Ben
Jonson's chosen type or example of high-minded
innocence, incessantly pursued by malice, delated
and defamed, but always triumphant and confident,
even when driven to the verge of a precipice, is
none other than Ben Jonson. His accusers were
'great ones'; but they 'were driven, for want of
crimes, to use invention, which was found slander ;
or too late (being entered so far) to seek starting-
holes for their rashness, which were not given them.'

His profession also, as well as his person, was attacked: 'they objected making of verses to me when I could object to most of them their not being able to read them but as worthy of scorn'; and strove, after the changeless manner of their estimable kind, to back and bolster up their accusations and objections by falsified and garbled extracts, 'which was an excellent way of malice; as if any man's context might not seem dangerous and offensive, if that which was knit to what went before were defrauded of his beginning; or that things by themselves uttered might not seem subject to calumny, which read entire would appear most free.' So little difference is there, in the composition of the meanest and foolishest among literary parasites and backbiters, between the characteristic developments or the representative products of the seventeenth and the nineteenth century.

At last they would object to me my poverty: I confess she is my domestic; sober of diet, simple of habit, frugal, painful, a good counsellor to me, that keeps me from cruelty, pride, or other more delicate impertinences, which are the nurse-children of riches.

All 'great and monstrous wickednesses,' avers the Laureate—not perhaps without an implied reference to such hideous instances as the case of

Somerset and Overbury,—' are the issue of the wealthy giants and the mighty hunters : whereas no great work, or worthy of praise or memory, but came out of poor cradles. It was the ancient poverty that founded commonweals, built cities, invented arts, made wholesome laws, armed men against vices, rewarded them with their own virtues, and preserved the honour and state of nations, till they betrayed themselves to riches.'

It is hardly too much to say that there are few finer passages than that in Landor ; in other words, that there can be few passages as fine in any third writer of English prose.

The fierce and severe attack on worldliness and love of money which follows this noble panegyric on the virtues of poverty should be read as part of the same essay rather than as a separate note or reflection. Indeed, throughout the latter part of the *Discoveries*, it is obvious that we have before us the fragments, disunited and disjointed, of single and continuous essays on various great subjects, rather than the finished and coherent works which their author would have offered to his readers had he lived long enough in health and strength of spirit and of body to carry out his original design. This sermon against greed of all kinds—avarice, luxury,

ambition of state and magnificence of expenditure
—is full of lofty wisdom and of memorable
eloquence.

What a wretchedness is this, to thrust all our riches
outward, and be beggars within ; to contemplate nothing
but the little, vile, and sordid things of the world : not
the great, noble, and precious? We serve our avarice ;
and not content with the good of the earth that is offered
us, we search and dig for the evil that is hidden. God
offered us those things, and placed them at hand and
near us, that he knew were profitable for us; but the
hurtful he laid deep and hid. Yet do we covet only the
things whereby we may perish ; and bring them forth,
when God and nature hath buried them. We covet superfluous things, when it were more honour for us if we could
contemn necessary.

A little further on, the Laureate who had lavished
the wealth of his poetic invention and his scenic
ingenuity on the festivities which welcomed the
Danish king to the court of his brother-in-law
refers in the following terms of sorrowful and
sarcastic reminiscence to those splendid and sterile
extravagances of meaningless magnificence.

Have I not seen the pomp of a whole kingdom, and
what a foreign king could bring hither? all[1] to make

[1] The current text reads 'Also' ! My emendation at all events
makes sense of a fine passage.

himself gazed and wondered at, laid forth as it were to
the show—and vanish all away in a day. And shall that
which could not fill the expectation of few hours enter-
tain and take up our whole lives? when even it appeared
as superfluous to the possessors as to me that was a
spectator. The bravery was shown, it was not possessed:
while it boasted itself, it perished. It is vile, and a poor
thing, to place our happiness on these desires. Say we
wanted them all. Famine ends famine.

These reflections are uncourtly enough from
the hand of a courtly poet ; but they are tame and
tender if compared with his animadversions on ' vice
and deformity,' which ' we may behold—so much
the fouler in having all the splendour of riches to
gild them, or the false light of honour and power
to help them. Yet this is that wherewith the world
is taken, and runs mad to gaze on : clothes and
titles, the birdlime of fools.'

No man ever made more generous response to
the friendly or generous kindness of others than
Ben Jonson : no man had ever less disposition or
inclination towards the grudging mood of mind
which regrets or the abject mood of mind which
resents the acceptance of a benefit. For all that
he received of help or support from his wealthier
friends or patrons he returned the noblest and
most liberal payment in manly and self-respectful

gratitude : he did not, like the rival poets of the restored Stuarts, condescend to undertake the deification or glorification of a male or female prostitute of parliament or of court : but it must be admitted that the outpourings of his heart in thanks and praises may seem somewhat excessive even to those who bear in mind that the tribute of his cordial homage was by no means confined to kings and princes, lords and ladies. But that ' he would not flatter Neptune for his trident or Jove for his power to thunder '—that he would not speak well, that he could hardly forbear from speaking evil, of any whom he found or whom he held to be undeserving—is as certain as that no loftier scorn than breathes through the words above transcribed was ever expressed by the most democratic or sarcastic of republicans for the mere attributes of rank and power. This fierce and deep contempt informs with even more vehement eloquence the note which follows.

What petty things they are we wonder at ! like children, that esteem every trifle, and prefer a fairing before their fathers ; what difference is betwixt us and them, but that we are dearer fools, coxcombs at a higher rate ? . . . All that we call happiness is mere painting and gilt ; and all for money : what a thin membrane of honour that is ! and how hath all true reputation fallen, since money began to have any! Yet the great herd, the multitude, that in all other things are divided, in this alone conspire and agree; to love money. They wish for it, they embrace it, they adore it : while yet it is possest with greater stir and torment than it was gotten.

The pure and lofty wisdom of the next note is worthy of Epictetus or Aurelius.

Some men, what losses soever they have, they make them greater : and if they have none, even all that is not gotten is a loss. Can there be creatures of more wretched condition than these, that continually labour under their own misery and others' envy?[1] A man should study other things : not to covet, not to fear, not to repent him : to make his base such as no tempest shall shake him : to be secure of all opinion, and pleasing to himself, even for that wherein he displeases others : for the worst opinion, gotten for doing well, should delight us. Wouldst not thou be just but for fame, thou oughtest to be it with infamy : he that would have his virtue published is not the servant of virtue, but glory.

In the following satirical observation all students will recognize the creator of Fastidious Brisk—and rather, perhaps, the spirit of Macilente than of Asper.

A dejected countenance, and mean clothes, beget

That is, the envy they bear towards others: an equivocal, awkward, and affected Latinism. The writer would not—he never would—remember that a phrase or a construction which makes very good Latin may make very bad English.

often a contempt, but it is with the shallowest creatures ; courtiers commonly : look up even with them in a new suit, you get above them straight. Nothing is more short-lived than [? their] pride : it is but while their clothes last : stay but while these are worn out, you cannot wish the thing more wretched or dejected.

In the four notes which compose a brief essay on painting (or, as Jonson calls it, picture) the finest passage by far is this wise and noble word of tribute paid to another great art by a great artist in letters :—

Whosoever loves not picture is injurious to truth and all the wisdom of poetry. Picture is the invention of heaven, the most ancient, and most akin to nature. It is itself a silent work, and always of one and the same habit : yet it doth so enter and penetrate the inmost affection (being done by an excellent artificer) as sometimes it overcomes the power of speech and oratory.

The summary history of ' picture,' or the art of painting, in which Jonson has given us his views on the relation of that art to poetry, geometry, optics, and moral philosophy, bears no less witness to his wide reading and his painstaking attention than to his quaint and dogmatic self-confidence in laying down the law at second hand on subjects of which he seems to have known less than little. But when we pass from criticism of painters to the lower ground of satirical observation—from the heights of a noble art to the depths or levels of ignoble nature, we meet once more the same fierce and earnest critic of life who should certainly be acknowledged as the greatest of all poets by any one—if any one there be — to whom 'criticism of life' seems acceptable or imaginable as a definition of the essence or the end of poetry.

The opening of the satirical essay on parasites which is here divided or split up into two sections by the blundering negligence and the unprincipled incompetence of its editors has the force and the point of a keen and heavy weapon, edged with wit and weighted with indignation. Juvenal has hardly left us a more vivid likeness of the creatures who 'grow suspected of the master, hated of the servants, while they inquire, and reprehend, and compound, and delate business of the house they have nothing to do with.' This note ends with the admirable remark, 'I know not truly which is worse, he that maligns all or that praises all.' An eminent poet and dramatist of our own age, M. Auguste Vacquerie, has said much the same thing in words even more terse, accurate, and forcible than Jonson's :—' Louer tout, c'est une autre façon de dénigrer tout.'

What follows as part of the same note is a letter to a nobleman who had asked Jonson's advice as to the education of his sons, 'and especially to the advancement of their studies.' The kindly and practical wisdom of his counsel is 'not of an age, but for all time': indeed, it is in some points as far ahead of our own age as of the writer's. Though nature 'be proner in some children to some disciplines, yet are they naturally prompt to taste all by degrees, and with change. For change is a kind of refreshing in studies, and infuseth knowledge by way of recreation.' The old Westminster boy, who had paid such loyal homage of gratitude to the ' most reverend head ' of his old master, is as emphatic in his preference of public to private education as in his insistence that scholars ' should not be affrighted or deterred in their entry, but drawn on with exercise and emulation.' His illustrious namesake of the succeeding century was hardly more emphatic in his advocacy of the opposite principle. That which Samuel Johnson and Charles Kingsley considered as ' doubtless the best of all punishments ' is denounced by Ben Jonson as energetically as by Quintilian : but I trust he would not have preferred to it the execrable modern substitute of torture by transcription—the infernal and idiotic infliction of so many hundred lines to be written out by way of penance.

Would we did not spoil our own children, and over-throw their manners ourselves by too much indulgence! To breed them at home is to breed them in a shade; where in a school they have the light and heat of the sun. They are used and accustomed to things and men. When they come forth into the commonwealth, they find nothing new, or to seek. They have made their friendships and aids, some to last their age. They hear what is commanded to others as well as themselves. Much approved, much corrected; all which they bring to their own store and use, and learn as much as they hear. Eloquence would be but a poor thing if we did but converse with singulars—speak man and man together. Therefore I like no private breeding. I would send them where their industry should be daily increased by praise; and that kindled by emulation. It is a good thing to inflame the mind, and though ambition itself be a vice, it is often the cause of great virtue. Give me that wit whom praise excites, glory puts on, or disgrace grieves; he is to be nourished with ambition, pricked forward with honour, checked with reprehension, and never to be suspected of sloth. Though he be given to play, it is a sign of spirit and liveliness, so there be a mean had of their sports and relaxations.

If the nineteenth century has said anything on this subject as well worth hearing—as wise, as humane, as reasonable, as full of sympathy and of judgment—as these reflections and animadversions of a scholar living in the first half or quarter of the seventeenth, I have never chanced to meet with it.

The forty-eight notes or entries which complete the sum of Ben Jonson's *Discoveries* should be considered as composing an essay on style, continuous in aim though desultory in treatment. The cruel, stupid, and insolent neglect of his editors has left it in so disjointed and dislocated a condition that we can only read it as we might read so many stray notes jotted down irregularly at odd moments on the first sheet or scrap of paper which might have fallen under the fatigued and fitful hand of the venerable poet.   The very last entry is a repetition of a former remark and a former quotation, tumbled in by some blundering printer's devil with no reference whatever to the sentence preceding it.[1]   As to the punctuation, let one example stand for many.   'Again, whether a man's genius is best able to reach thither, it should more and more contend, lift, and dilate itself.'   To rectify this hopeless nonsense does not require the skill of a Bentley or a Porson.   It is obvious that Jonson must have written ' whither a man's genius is best able to

---

[1] Compare lxxii., *Not.* 4, and clxxi.

reach, thither,' &c. But the moles and bats who have hitherto taken charge of this great writer's text could not see even so simple and glaring a fact as this.

It is natural that Jonson should insist with some excess of urgency on the necessity for care and labour in writing.

No matter how slow the style be at first, so it be laboured and accurate : seek the best, and be not glad of the froward conceits or first words that offer themselves to us ; but judge of what we invent, and order what we approve. Repeat often what we have formerly written ; which beside that it helps the consequence, and makes the juncture better, it quickens the heat of imagination, that often cools in the time of setting down, and gives it new strength, as if it grew lustier by the going back. As we see in the contention of leaping, they jump farthest that fetch their race largest; or as in throwing a dart or javelin we force back our arms to make our loose the stronger. Yet, if we have a fair gale of wind, I forbid not the steering out of our sail, so the favour of the gale deceive us not. For all that we invent doth please us in the conception or birth, else we would never set it down.

This extract is no exceptional example of the purity, force, and weight of style by which this essay is distinguished even among the works of its author. It is impossible for any commentator to

convey more than a most imperfect impression of
its rich and various merits.

Great as was Jonson's reliance on the results of
training and study, he never forgot that 'arts and
precept avail nothing, except nature be beneficial
and aiding. And therefore these things are no
more written to a dull disposition than rules of
husbandry to a barren soil. No precepts will
profit a fool ; no more than beauty will the
blind, or music the deaf. As we should take care
that our style in writing be neither dry nor empty,
we should look again it be not winding, or wanton
with far-fetched descriptions: either is a vice. But
that is worse which proceeds out of want than
that which riots out of plenty. The remedy of
fruitfulness is easy, but no labour will help the
contrary.'

Of Spenser, whom he seems to have liked no
better than did Landor—in other words, no better
than might have been expected of him,—he
speaks here, on one point at least, in terms quite
opposite to those recorded in Drummond's too
sparing and irregular but delightful and in-
valuable notes. To the Scottish poet he said
that 'Spenser's stanzas pleased him not, nor his
matter ': whereas in this later essay, while still

insisting that 'Spenser, in affecting the ancients, writ no language,' he adds, 'yet I would have him read for his matter, but as Virgil read Ennius.' In his preference of Plautus to Terence, it may be observed that Ben Jonson anticipated the verdict of two such very different great men as Jonathan Swift and Victor Hugo.

In the Greek poets, as also in Plautus, we shall see the economy and disposition of poems better observed than in Terence, and the latter [that is, in later comic dramatists], who thought the sole grace and virtue of their fable the sticking in of sentences, as ours do the forcing in of jests.

The Herculean energy and industry of Jonson might have been expected to make him as intolerant of indolence as he shows himself in the following fine passage :—

We should not protect our sloth with the patronage of difficulty. It is a false quarrel [*querela*, as the marginal title of this note expresses it] against nature, that she helps understanding but in a few, when the most part of mankind are inclined by her thither, if they would take the pains ; no less than birds to fly, horses to run, &c. ; which if they lose, it is through their own sluggishness, and by that means become her prodigies, not her children.

The whole of the section which opens with these noble and fervent words should be most carefully studied by those who would appreciate the peculiar character of Jonson's intelligence and genius. It may be doubted, even by those who would admit that we learn best what we learn earliest, whether 'nature in children is more patient of labour in study, than in age; for the sense of the pain, the labour of the judgment, is absent; they do not measure what they have done. And it is the thought and consideration that affects us, more than the weariness itself.' Plato, we are reminded, went first to Italy and afterwards to Egypt in pursuit of Pythagorean and Osirian mysteries. 'He laboured, so must we.' From the examples of musicians and preachers, whose work requires the service of many faculties at once, this lesson may be drawn :—'if we can express this variety together, why should not divers studies, at divers hours, delight, when the variety is able alone to refresh and repair us? As, when a man is weary of writing, to read ; and then again of reading, to write. Wherein, howsoever we do many things, yet are we (in a sort) still fresh to what we begin ; we are recreated with change, as the stomach is with meats. . . . It is easier to do many things, and continue, than to do one thing long.'

'A fool may talk,' as Jonson observes a little further on, 'but a wise man speaks': and to such a man it will scarcely be questioned that we have been listening. But though 'it were a sluggish and base thing to despair' when the attainment of knowledge is possible, yet, 'if a man should prosecute as much as could be said of everything, his work would find no end.'

The next four notes deal more directly with special and practical details and principles of style. If some of the points insisted on seem either obsolete or obvious, there are others which cannot be too often asserted or too strenuously maintained. Silence may be golden on certain occasions; but it is none the less certain that 'speech is the only benefit man hath to express his excellency of mind above other creatures. Words are the people's, yet there is a choice of them to be made'; and the rules laid down for the limitation and regulation of this choice are as sound in principle as brilliant in expression. At every step we find something which might well be quoted in evidence of this.

A good man always profits by his endeavour, by his

help, yea, when he is absent, nay, when he is dead, by
his example and memory.   So good authors in their style :
a strict and succinct style is that where you can take
away nothing without loss, and that loss to be manifest.

The grace of metaphor in the following sentence is not more notable than the soundness of
its counsel.

Some words are to be culled out for ornament and
colour, as we gather flowers to strew houses, or make
garlands ; but they are better when they grow in our style ;
as in a meadow, where though the mere grass and green-
ness delight, yet the variety of flowers doth heighten and
beautify.

No modern student of letters will read this
without seeing in it an anticipatory tribute to the
incomparable style of Mr. Ruskin.

All the definitions of different styles are good,
but this is excellent :—

The congruent and harmonious fitting of parts in a
sentence hath almost the fastening and force of knitting
and connection ; as in stones well squared, which will
rise strong a great way without mortar.

The reader of the following extract will be
reminded at its close of an ever-memorable deliverance recorded by Boswell.

Periods are beautiful, when they are not too long ; for

so they have their strength too, as in a pike or javelin.
As we must take the care that our words and sense be
clear, so, if the obscurity happen through the hearer's or
reader's want of understanding, I am not to answer for
them, no more than for their not listening or marking ;
I must neither find them ears nor mind.

All must remember how the second great
dictator of literary London who bore the name of
Johnson expressed the same very rational objec-
tion :—' I have found you a reason, sir ; I am not
bound to find you an understanding.'

The following precept is of perennial value—
and of perennial application.

We should therefore speak what we can the nearest
way, so as we keep our gait, not leap ; for too short may
as well be not let into the memory, as too long not kept
in. Whatsoever loseth the grace and clearness, converts
into a riddle : the obscurity is marked, but not the value.
That perisheth, and is passed by, like the pearl in the
fable. Our style should be like a skein of silk, to be
carried and found by the right thread, not ravelled and
perplexed : then all is a knot, a heap.

Nor is this less weighty or less true :—

Language most shows a man. Speak, that I may see
thee. It springs out of the most retired and inmost parts of
us, and is the image of the parent of it, the mind. No glass
renders a man's form or likeness so true as his speech.

Nay, it is likened to a man : and as we consider feature and composition in a man, so words in language ; in the greatness, aptness, sound, structure, and harmony of it.

The seven succeeding notes deal in more detail with various kinds of oratory ; 'high and great,' 'grave, sinewy, and strong,' or 'humble and low,' ,plain and pleasing,' or 'vicious' and bombastic, 'fleshy, fat, and corpulent—full of suet and tallow,' or 'bony and sinewy.' These notes are as full of happy and humorous illustration as of sound and sensible criticism ; but it is a matter of more interest to consider the observations of such a man as Jonson on such men as Bacon and Aristotle. His reflections on the mediæval worship of a name are not unworthy of modern consideration.

Nothing is more ridiculous than to make an author a dictator, as the schools have done Aristotle. The damage is infinite knowledge receives by it : for to many things a man should owe but a temporary relief and suspension of his own judgment, not an absolute resignation of himself, or a perpetual captivity. Let Aristotle and others have their dues ; but if we can make farther discoveries of truth and fitness than they, why are we envied? Let us beware, while we strive to add, we do not diminish or deface ; we may improve, but not augment. By discrediting falsehood, truth grows in request. We must not go about, like men anguished or perplexed, for vicious affectation of praise ; but calmly study the separation of opinions, find the errors have intervened, awake antiquity, call former times into question ; but make no parties with the present, nor follow any fierce undertakers ; mingle no matter of doubtful credit with the simplicity of truth, but gently stir the mould about the root of the question.

The remarks ' on epistolary style ' are rich in humour and good sense, as well as curiously illustrative of the singular fashion of the time. 'Sometimes men make baseness of kindness,' observes the writer ; and proceeds to illustrate the fact, in a manner which may remind us of Thackeray's, by examples of absurd and verbose adulation, expressed in phrases ' that go a-begging for some meaning, and labour to be delivered of the great burden of nothing.'

A word seems to have dropped out of the following admirable sentence ; but the beetle-headed boobies to whose carelessness the charge of Jonson's posthumous writings was committed by the malignity of accident were incapable of noticing the nonsense they had made of it.

The next property of epistolary style is perspicuity, and is oftentimes [lost] by affectation of some wit ill angled for, or ostentation of some hidden terms of art. Few words they darken speech, and so do too many ; as well too much light hurteth the eyes as too little ; and a long bill of chancery confounds the understanding as much as the shortest note ; therefore let not your letters be penned like English statutes, and this is obtained.

Passing from the subjects of oratory and letter-writing to the subject of poetry, the Laureate at once falls foul of his personal assailants. ' The age is grown so tender of her fame, as she calls all writings aspersions. That is the state word, the phrase of court—Placentia College, which some call Parasites' Place, the Inn of Ignorance.' That is a tolerably harsh phrase for a wearer of courtly laurels to allow himself ; but it is gentle and temperate compared with this effusion of divine wrath on the heads of victims now indiscernible and secure from fame or shame.

It sufficeth I know what kind of persons I displease ; men bred in the declining and decay of virtue, betrothed to their own vices ; that have abandoned or prostituted their good names ; hungry and ambitious of infamy, invested in all deformity, enthralled to ignorance and malice, of a hidden and concealed malignity, and that hold a concomitancy with all evil.

The general and historical notes on poetry which follow are of less interest than they assuredly must have been if Jonson had given us

less of Aristotle, Cicero, and Horace, and more
of himself. It is therefore less important to know
what he thought of Euripides than to know what
he thought of Aristotle.

But whatsoever nature at any time dictated to the
most happy, or long exercise to the most laborious, that
the wisdom and learning of Aristotle hath brought into
an art ; because he understood the causes of things : and
what other men did by chance or custom, he doth by
reason ; and not only found out the way not to err, but
the short way we should take not to err.

' To judge of poets,' says a later note, ' is only
the faculty of poets ; and not of all poets, but the
best.' It is unlucky that in the note preceding it
Ben Jonson should have committed himself to the
assertion that Euripides, of all men, ' is sometimes
peccant, as he is most times perfect.' The perfection of such shapeless and soulless abortions as
the *Phœnissae* and the *Hercules Furens* is about as
demonstrable as the lack of art which Ben Jonson
regretted and condemned in the author of *Hamlet*
and *Othello*.

It is comically pathetic to find that the failure
of Jonson's later comedies had led him to observe,
with the judicious Aristotle, that ' the moving of
laughter is a fault in comedy, a kind of turpitude

that depraves some part of a man's nature without a disease ' : and likewise that 'this induced Plato to esteem of Homer as a sacrilegious person, because he presented the gods sometimes laughing.' But this deplorable and degrading instinct of perverse humanity becomes irrepressible and irresistible in the reader who discovers in the author of *Bartholomew Fair* and *The Silent Woman* so delicate and sensitive a dislike of plebeian horseplay and farcical scurrility that he cannot at any price abide the insolence and indecency of so vulgar a writer as Aristophanes.

The concluding essay on 'the magnitude and compass of any fable, epic or dramatic,' is of less interest, except to special students, than the animadversions of the writer on more particular subjects of criticism. Constant good sense, occasional felicity of expression, conscientious and logical intensity of application or devotion to every point of the subject handled or attempted, all readers will find, as all readers will expect : and it should be superfluous to repeat that they will find a text so corrupt and so confused as no editor of any but an English classic would venture to publish.

And now it must be evident that if Ben

Jonson was the author of Bacon's Essays— as that eminent Irish-American scholar, Dr. Athanasius Dogberry (of New Gotham, U.S.A.), maintains with a fervour not unworthy of Rabbi Zeal-of-the-Land Busy—his genius and his intelligence were by no means at their best when he produced that famous volume, and gave or sold it to his friend the Lord Chancellor. The full and fertile harvest of eloquence and thought, the condensed and compressed wealth of reflection and observation, overflowing on all sides from the narrow garner or treasury of the wonderful little book on which I have not hoped to write anything more than a most imperfect and inadequate commentary, may still be left unreaped and untreasured by the common cry of nominal students or lovers of English literature. But none who have studied it can fail to recognize that its author was in every way worthy to have been the friend of Bacon and of Shakespeare.

TEXTUAL NOTES

THE following notes list all printing variations of the London issue (Chatto and Windus, 1889)—designated here as L—from the New York issue (Worthington Co., 1889), reproduced as the text of this edition. These notes also record substantive, punctuation, and spelling variations of the periodical publication from this text; Part I was first printed in *The Nineteenth Century,* XXIII (1888), 603–616 (April) and 693–715 (May)—designated here as NC—and Parts II and III first appeared in *The Fortnightly Review,* L(o.s.)(1888), 24–38 (July) and 425–447 (October), respectively—designated here as FR. The numbers on the left identify page and line numbers, respectively. Omission of a siglum after the bracket indicates that the publication in question agrees with the reading of the text.

1.2. TRAGEDIES,] TRAGEDIES L.

6.19. nature;] nature: NC.

6.26. conscience;] conscience: NC.

13.25–26. unite . . . of] combine to produce and succeed in producing NC.

14.7. *The Fox*] *Volpone* NC.

18. p. # 18] *vertical spacing of 1 varies in* L.

19.25. merits;] merits: NC.

20.24–25. studiously . . . laboriously] tediously brilliant and studiously NC.

23.10–11. *Line settings vary in* L.

23.20. last] last, NC.

29.3. sympathy;] sympathy: NC.

35.16. serious] tragic NC.

38.5. masterpiece,] masterpiece L.

42.10. comedy;] comedy: NC.

47.26.   *Spacing on left margin varies in* L.

49.3–4.   *Line settings vary in* L.

50.26.   industrious] pure NC.

51.21.   intolerant:] intolerant; L.

55.17.   now] yet NC.

60.26.   the admiration] he admiration L.

62.15.   incongruity;] incongruity: NC.

63.17.   intention;] intention: NC.

63.18.   under-current] undercurrent NC.

72.4.   dexterity,] dèxterity NC.

73.5.   to] by NC.

73.13.   Dumas.] Dumas NC.

74.26.   least] east L.

75.23.   personifications;] personifications: NC.

80.14.   Masque,'] Masque, L.

80.20.   collapse.] collapse L.

82.19.   fairer] better NC.

83.1–4.   *Spacing on left margin varies in* L.

83.   Sig. # G2] *upside down in* L.

84.12.   to 't;'] to 't'; NC.

84.16.   ètreint;'] ètreint'; L *and* NC.

85.27.   *Appears as first line of type on p. 86 in* L.

86.26.   *Appears as first line of type on p. 87 in* L.

87.26.   *Appears as first line of type on p. 88 in* L.

88.26.   *Appears as first line of type on p. 89 in* L.

89.21.   song;] song: NC.

93.1.   Shake-] Shake L.

94.12.   cedes.] cedes FR.

94.19.   plura':] plura:" FR. *Double quotation marks are used throughout* The Fortnightly Review *for quotations where single quotation marks are used in both the London and New York printings.*

96.16.   *The New Cry,*] "The New Cry," FR.

96.20. talk] "talk FR. *Double quotation marks are used throughout* The Fortnightly Review *for indented quotations where no quotation marks are used in either the London or New York printings.*

98.7. recognize] recognise FR.

98.12. shone down] eclipsed FR.

99.18. series called] series of fifteen lyric or elegiac poems called FR.

100.15. avowal] confession FR.

100.21. own] *omitted* FR.

100.22. acknow-] acknow FR.

101.28. ¹In] (1) In FR. *This difference in footnote numbering at the bottom of the page continues throughout* The Fortnightly Review.

102.5. forbears;] forbears L.

103.19. but] but, FR.

110.12. all';] all;" FR.

111.17. truth] fact FR.

112.11. insensibility,] insensibility FR.

113.7. 'The] The L.

113.10-11. *The following paragraphs printed in* The Fortnightly Review *between these, concluding line 10, and* The version, *beginning line 11, are omitted in both the London and New York printings:*

In a later part of the translation there is an obvious and preposterous misprint which would suggest that even the devoted Gifford cannot have thought it worth while to revise the text of this unlucky poem—which in that case, it seems to me, he should not have undertaken to edit. This is what Horace says (as "every schoolboy" on whom the study of that versifier has been inflicted knows only too well):—

"Intererit multùm Davusne loquatur an heros."

And this is how the printers represent Ben Jonson as construing that not very difficult line:—

"It much will differ if a god speak, than,
Or an heroë."

Now even in those early days when Jonson was capable of writing *than* for *then* and *heroë* for *hero* he cannot have been capable of taking Davus for a deity. Yet all his editors have overlooked the obvious misprint of "god" for "clod"; not the only gross and palpable error in the course of a few pages.

123.14.   Light';] Light;" FR.

124.21.   comedy;] comedy: FR.

124.23.   *Humour*:] *Humour*; FR.

129.19.   dry] dry, FR.

132.8.   dry:] dry; FR.

133.23–25.   [in . . . elicit']] (in . . . elicit") FR.

133.25.   I am] "I am FR.

136.23.   written:] written; FR.

137.25–26.   [was . . . these?]] (was . . . these?) FR.

139.3.   will] will, FR.

141.6.   ing';] ing;" FR.

141.23.   seen';] seen;" FR.

144.2.   thefts;'] thefts"; FR.

144.4.   arts] arts" FR.

146.24.   interes] interest FR.

147.22.   his] is L.

148.9–10.   *Line settings vary in* L.

148.25.   'Why] Why L.

150.9.   men] men, L *and* FR.

150.23.   play,] play; FR.

150.26.   *Vertical spacing varies in* L.

153.15.   the boughs] t   boughs FR.
153.16.   enemies] enemie FR.
153.17.   when] whe FR.
154.13.   [qu. counsel?]] (qu. counsel?) FR.
158.2.   me] me, FR.
158.4.   scorn';] scorn; L; scorn;" FR.
158.25.   Laureate] laureate FR.
160.6.   world:] world; FR.
171.10–11.   [that . . . dramatists],] "(that . . . dramatists)," FR.
171.19–20.   [*querela* . . . it]] "(*querela* . . . it)" FR.
173.4.   speaks':] speaks:" FR.
176.7.   ,plain] 'plain L; "plain FR.
176.19.   relief] belief FR.
178.6.   Laureate] laureate FR.
180.2.   disease':] disease:" FR.

EXPLANATORY NOTES

REFERENCES to Jonson's works in the notes are to the modern standard edition, *Ben Jonson*, ed. C. H. Herford, Percy and Elizabeth Simpson, 11 vols. (London, 1925–52), except where Swinburne refers specifically to the edition of Jonson he used, *The Works of Ben Jonson*, ed. W. Gifford, rev. by F. Cunningham, 9 vols. (London, 1875)—hereafter cited as *Works*. Quotations from Jonson are identified only when the reference may not appear clear in the context. References to Swinburne's works are to *The Complete Works of Algernon Charles Swinburne*, ed. Sir Edmund Gosse and Thomas J. Wise, 20 vols. (London, 1925–27)—known as the Bonchurch Edition—unless otherwise indicated. Numbers at the left refer to pages of the text of this volume.

3. Enceladus. The most powerful of the hundred-armed giants who were defeated by Zeus (Jupiter) in the war with the Titans.

3. Cartwright, William (1611–1643), and Randolph, Thomas (1605–1635), were particularly adoring "sons of Ben." See their poems on Jonson, Herford and Simpson, XI, 390–396, and 455–459.

3. Gilchrist, Octavius (1779–1823), published two pamphlets defending Jonson against unfriendly critics: *An Examination of the Charges Maintained by Messrs. Malone, Chalmers, and Others, of Ben Jonson's Enmity, &c. towards Shakespeare* (London, 1808) and *A Letter to William Gifford, Esq. on the Late Edition of Ford's Plays; Chiefly as Relating to Ben Jonson* (London, 1811).

5. lyrical verses . . . Drummond. Swinburne is apparently referring to the song "To Celia," which begins "Drinke to me, onely, with thine eyes," printed in *The*

Forest as the ninth poem, and to the seventh poem in "A Celebration of Charis," beginning "For *Loves*-sake, kisse me once againe," printed in *The Underwood*, though Jonson does not declare them to be "his best." Cf. *Conversations with Drummond*, ll. 94–101.

5. incantation in *Œdipus*. John Dryden and Nathaniel Lee's *Oedipus*, III.i. The incantation is reputed to be wholly by Dryden.

5. incantation in *Manfred*. I.i.192–261. The first four stanzas would include ll. 192–231.

7. axiom . . . art-critic. The "famous axiom" is that the picture would have been better if the artist had taken more pains, but a search of Goldsmith's works failed to reveal it there. The idea is commonplace, and since Swinburne is apparently relying on his memory, he may well be mistaken as to the source.

10. *Sir John Oldcastle* (1599) was written by Michael Drayton, Richard Hathway, Anthony Munday, and Robert Wilson, but in an edition dated 1600 the author is declared to be Shakespeare. See E. K. Chambers, *The Elizabethan Stage* (London, 1923), III, 306–307.

11. slave-dealer and slave-driver. Philip Henslowe, the theatrical entrepreneur whose famous "diary" records payments to the stable of writers in his employ between 1592 and 1603. See Chambers, *The Elizabethan Stage*, I, 360–376.

12. 'Plautinos . . . sales': "both the measures and the wit of Plautus" (Horace, *Ars Poetica*, ll. 270–271 [Loeb ed.]). Horace's contempt for the coarseness and meter of Plautus is indicated in the context of the quotation (ll. 270–274).

12. defence of poetry. *Every Man in his Humour* (1601 Q), V.v.312–343.

15. remarks of Gifford. *Works*, I, liii–lxv.

19. final verse . . . epilogue. *"By (---) 'tis good, and if you lik't, you may."*

25. Shakespeare . . . 'wanted art.' *Conversations with Drummond*, 1. 50.

27. error of . . . Martha. Martha, sister of Mary, was too busy with household chores to hear the words of Jesus (Luke 10:38–42).

28. Coleridge . . . Arruntius. Cf. Coleridge's note on *Sejanus*, I.244–254, in *Coleridge's Miscellaneous Criticism*, ed. Thomas Middleton Raysor (Cambridge, Mass., 1936), p. 53.

29. *Si . . . flere*: "If you wish me to weep." The sentence continues, "dolendum est/ Primum ipsi tibi": "you must first feel pain yourself" (Horace, *Ars Poetica*, 1. 102).

32. Coleridge . . . presage. Cf. Coleridge's note on *Sejanus*, V.i, in *Miscellaneous Criticism*, ed. Raysor, p. 54.

32. acclaimed by Chapman. Chapman contributed verses which were prefixed to the quarto publication of *Sejanus* in 1605; these are reprinted in Herford and Simpson, XI, 309–313.

34. *Panegyre* . . . Gifford. Cf. *Works*, VI, 437.

37. Scapin or Mascarille. Scheming servants in Molière's plays: Scapin in *Les Fourberies de Scapin* and Mascarille in *L'Etourdi ou Les contre-temps* and in *Dépit amoureaux*.

38. uncle Toby. The allusion is to both Sir Toby Belch in *Twelfth Night* and Uncle Toby in Sterne's *Tristram Shandy*.

38. Sir John Brute. The provoking husband in John Vanbrugh's play *The Provok'd Wife*.

38. Mr. Peggotty. A rough-hewn but kind fisherman in Dickens' *David Copperfield*.

38. Lady Wishfort. A lecherous dowager in William Congreve's play *The Way of the World*.

38. Lady Kew. The authoritarian but witty Countess Dowager of Kew in Thackeray's *The Newcomes*.

38. Sir Sampson Legend. The boorish father who is outwitted by his sons in Congreve's *Love for Love*.

39. Sir Wilful Witwoud. A country bumpkin in Congreve's *The Way of the World*. The particular allusion is to III.iii.

39. modern master of analytic art. Swinburne is apparently referring to Robert Browning, whom he greatly admired. Cf. Swinburne's discussion of the "analytic genius" of Browning in his study of George Chapman, Bonchurch XII, 145–155.

40. study of Sludge. Robert Browning's "Mr. Sludge, 'The Medium'," a dramatic portrait of a spiritualist, published in *Dramatis Personae* (1864).

40. Coleridge . . . 'planned.' *Table Talk* (July 5, 1834) in *Miscellaneous Criticism*, ed. Raysor, p. 437.

41. Gifford's . . . 'intellect.' Cf. Gifford's note on "*The Fox*" (*Works*, III, 322), but the phrase is applied only to *The Alchemist* by Gifford.

42. lion . . . fox. Qualities of the Machiavell. Cf. Machiavelli, *The Prince*, XVIII.

42. foolish . . . rhyme. The anonymous seventeenth-century doggerel reads: "The Fox, the Alchemist, and Silent Woman,/ Done by Ben Jonson, and outdone by no man."

44. Ironside. Captain Ironside is a bluff soldier in *The Magnetic Lady*, but Swinburne may also be alluding to Oliver Cromwell, the Puritan leader and later gov-

ernor of the Commonwealth, who was called Ironside by the Royalists.

46. visit of King Christian. The king of Denmark, Queen Anne's brother, visited England in the summer of 1606.

46. whose temperance . . . Iago. *Othello*, II.iii.78–87.

46. Gifford's . . . commendation. Cf. *Works*, VI, 473.

46. mock marriage . . . Countess of Somerset. The Earl of Essex and Lady Frances Howard married in 1606, when the groom was fourteen and the bride thirteen. The Countess of Essex later obtained a divorce on the grounds that Essex was impotent and the marriage had not been consummated, though the Countess was suspected of drugging the Earl. The lady then married King James's current favorite, Robert Carr (or Ker), the newly created Earl of Somerset, in 1613 and was convicted in 1615 of poisoning Sir Thomas Overbury. For a discussion of these events, see G. P. V. Akrigg, *Jacobean Pageant, or the Court of King James I* (Cambridge, Mass., 1962), pp. 180–204.

47. Gifford . . . 'gem.' *Works*, VII, 69.

47. 'the divine original.' Catullus' poem on the marriage of Julia and Manilius, LXI, 152–201, which suggested ll. 477–506 of Jonson's masque.

47. 'well-torned and true-filed.' Jonson's description of Shakespeare's verse in Jonson's dedicatory poem prefixed to Shakespeare's First Folio (1623).

50. matter . . . of Molière's. Cf. Dryden's comment in his *Essay of Dramatic Poesy* that there is "more variety of them [humours] in some one play of Ben Johnson's, than in all of theirs [Molière, Corneille, Quinalt, 'and some others'] together," *Essays of John Dryden*, ed. W. P. Ker, I (Oxford, 1926), 68–69.

52. Gifford's . . . *Twelfth Night*. Cf. Gifford's note on IV.ii, *Works*, III, 436. Modern scholarship rejects the possibility of Shakespeare imitating Jonson in *Twelfth Night*, which is now generally regarded to have been written around the turn of the century, some eight years before *Epicoene*.

52. Dryden . . . record. Cf. Dryden's "Examen of the Silent Woman" in his *Essay of Dramatic Poesy, Essays*, ed. Ker, I, 83–88. Swinburne exaggerates Dryden's estimation of the play: Dryden says, "The intrigue of it is the greatest and most noble of any pure unmixed comedy in any language" (I, 83).

53. Ecclefechan. A village in Dumphriesshire, Scotland, the birthplace of Thomas Carlyle.

53. *malade imaginaire*. The hypocondriac Argan in Molière's *Le Malade imaginaire*.

53. Sganarelles. Sganarelle is the name of a major comic character in Molière's *Le Médicin malgre lui, Sganarelle ou Le cocu imaginaire*, and *L'École des maris*. Comic characters named Sganarelle appear also in Molière's *Dom Juan, L'Amour médicin*, and *Le Médicin volant*.

54. 'unequalled play.' Cf. Herrick, "*Upon* M. Ben Jonson. *Epig*." in *Hesperides*, reprinted in Herford and Simpson, XI, 488.

56. compliment . . . George Wither. Richard Barnfield (1574–1627) is particularly known for his amorous, mythological poetry of the 1590's, especially *The Affectionate Shepherd* (1594) and *Cynthia* (1595). George Wither (1588–1667) wrote pastoral, satiric, and elegiac poetry in the early seventeenth century; one of his most noted works is a book of eclogues entitled *The Shepherd's Hunting* (1615).

56. absurd misprint . . . 'any.' Swinburne's conjecture has been adopted by Herford and Simpson, VII, 371.

57. Coleridge . . . creature. Cf. Coleridge's note on I.505 ff. in *Miscellaneous Criticism*, ed. Raysor, p. 58.

57–58. famous definition . . . comedies. *Every Man out of his Humour*, Ind., ll. 88–114.

58. art . . . 'nature.' *The Winter's Tale*, IV.iv.97.

58. additions . . . to *The Spanish Tragedy*. Modern scholarship for the most part agrees with Swinburne, though the question remains unsettled. Cf. Herford and Simpson, II, 237–245.

60. his memoirs . . . 'birth.' *Works*, I, xc.

60. final note . . . 'The Alchemist.' *Works*, IV, 509.

60. Leigh Hunt . . . profusion. Hunt comments, Jonson "could not help consulting the worst taste" of his audience "and writing whole plays, like 'Bartholomew Fair,' full of the absolutest, and sometimes loathsomest, trash" ("Social Morality. Suckling and Ben Jonson," *Men, Women, and Books* [London, 1860], II, 13).

62. second nuptials . . . nullity. Lady Frances Howard married the Earl of Somerset in 1613 after her marriage to the Earl of Essex was nullified. See note to p. 46 above.

63. Rome under Pope Alexander VI. 1492–1503, a period notorious for ecclesiastical corruption and riotous living.

63. Paris under Queen Catherine de'Medici. Ca. 1560–1589, a time of religious wars, but also infamous for the intrigue and murder at court. This period of French history is represented by Marlowe in *The Massacre at Paris* and Chapman in his *Bussy D'Ambois* plays, which were imitated by Swinburne in his early tragedy,

The Queen Mother (with Catherine de'Medici as the title character), written "or sketched" while at Oxford between 1853 and 1859 (Sir Edmund Gosse, *The Life of Algernon Charles Swinburne*, Bonchurch XIX, 61) and published in 1860. The court societies of Pope Alexander VI and Catherine de'Medici are also compared by Swinburne in his article on Mary Stuart contributed to the *Encyclopaedia Britannica* (1883), reprinted in Bonchurch XIV, 376 ff.

66. Cathos . . . Bélise. Cathos and Madelon [Magdelon] are affected ladies who assume the fictitious names of Aminte and Polixène in Molière's *Les Précieuses ridicules*. Célimène and Arsinoè in *Le Misanthrope* and Philaminte and Bélise in *Les Femmes savantes* are Molière's representations of the same type.

67. "You . . . all." *The Devil is an Ass*, V.v.61–62.

69. 'tedious and brief.' Applied to the Pyramus and Thisbe "play" in *Midsummer Night's Dream*, V.i.58.

70. 'not of . . . all time.' "To the Memory of . . . Mr. William Shakespeare . . . ," l. 43, prefixed to Shakespeare's First Folio (1623).

76. Charles Surface. The prodigal who proves to be morally superior to his hypocritical brother Joseph in Sheridan's *The School for Scandal*.

76. Gifford . . . 'Bartholomew Fair.' Cf. Gifford's note on IV.i, *Works*, V, 248.

76. central 'Office' . . . 'spectators.' Cf. Jonson's note "To the Readers" prefacing Act III, ll. 1–7.

76. Gifford . . . 'audience.' *Works*, V, 220.

78. dialogues . . . Molière. Cf. Molière's *Critique de l'École des femmes* and *Impromptu de Versailles*, written in 1663 in defense of *L'École des femmes*.

78. Gifford . . . all. Cf. Gifford's note, which identifies the piece as "a mere monologue," *Works*, VIII, 52.

79. Lamb . . . 'bard.' *Specimens of English Dramatic Poets, Works of Charles and Mary Lamb*, ed. E. V. Lucas, IV (London, 1904), 265.

80. Dryden . . . 'dotages.' Dryden refers to Jonson's last plays as "dotages," *Essay of Dramatic Poesy, Essays*, ed. Ker, I, 81.

80. Sylvester, Joshua (1563–1618), translated Du Bartas and other French authors. He was praised by Jonson in *Epigrams*, CXXXII, but Jonson later commented that the translation of Du Bartas was "not well done," *Conversations with Drummond*, ll. 29–31. Sylvester's poetry is often flat and colloquial.

80. Quarles, Francis (1592–1644), is most famous for his *Emblems* (1635); his poetic style owes much to Sylvester's translation of Du Bartas.

81. Dryden . . . 'story.' *Essay of Dramatic Poesy, Essays,* ed. Ker, I, 65.

83. Dame Polish . . . Gifford. Cf. Gifford's note on V.x.84–100, *Works*, VI, 110–111.

83. 'not liked' . . . court. Sir Henry Herbert, Master of the Revels, records in his office-book that *A Tale of a Tub* was performed at court January 14, 1634, but was "not likte" (Herford and Simpson, I, 275).

83. Feltham's . . . 'nominal.' Cf. Owen Feltham's "An Answer to the Ode of Come leave the loathed Stage, &c.," ll. 21–22, reprinted in Herford and Simpson, XI, 339–340. Feltham is critical of Jonson's jest as "far beneath an able brain."

84. Mr. Dempster's . . . infamy. "Janet's repentance" (Chap. I) in *Scenes of Clerical Life*.

84. Miss Hoyden. A naive country girl and "great fortune" in Vanbrugh's *The Relapse*.

84. Miss Prue. A "simple" country girl in Congreve's *Love for Love*.

84. 'Qui . . . étreint': "Grasp all, lose all."

87–88. Gifford . . . ' "dress".' Cf. Gifford's note on *Poetaster*, III.iv.320–325, *Works*, II, 436.

88. Gifford's editorial enthusiasm. Cf. Gifford's note on the fragment, *Works*, VI, 228 and 287–288.

88. 'sovereign . . . masterdom.' *Macbeth*, I.v.71.

89. 'il maestro . . . sanno': "the master of them that know," applied by Dante to Aristotle (*The Divine Comedy, Inferno*, IV.131).

94. author . . . *The Bachelor's Banquet*. Thomas Dekker is the author of *The Gull's Hornbook*, but *The Bachelor's Banquet* is no longer accepted as Dekker's work.

94. 'It is' . . . 'selection.' *Works*, VIII, 142.

94. 'Sunt . . . plura': "Some are good, some are mediocre, and many are bad" (Martial, *Epigrams*, I.xvi).

94. 'not covetous' . . . 'phrase.' Jonson's second epigram, "To My Book."

95. Sir Walter Scott . . . 'nightmen.' *Life of Dryden, The Miscellaneous Prose Works* (Edinburgh, 1834–36), I, 277 n. Cf. "Essay on the Drama," *Miscellaneous Works*, VI, 338–342, and "Hawthornden" in *Provincial Antiquities, Miscellaneous Works*, VII, 374–382.

96. 'on Lucy Countess of Bedford' . . . admiration. *Works*, VIII, 185.

96. *gobemouche*: simpleton.

99. Macauley . . . 'rugged rhymes.' "Lord Bacon," *The Miscellaneous Works*, ed. Lady Trevelyan (New York, n.d.), IV, 76.

100. either . . . 'song-books.' *Lyrics from the Song-Books of the Elizabethan Age* (London, 1887) and *More Lyrics from the Song-Books of the Elizabethan Age* (London, 1888). Selected poems from the two volumes were published in a single volume in 1889.

100. Glover, Richard (1712–1785), wrote *Leonidas* (1737) in imitation of Milton; though Glover's epic attained a notable reputation in the eighteenth century, it has not stood the test of time.

100. satirist . . . 'Don.' The reference is apparently to Robert Buchanan who attacked Swinburne several times in reviews and articles (see my introduction, n. 23). Buchanan also was the author of some "amatory verses," particularly in *Ballads of Life, Love, and Humour* (1882). For Swinburne's scorn of Buchanan's critical and poetical ability, see "Notes on Poems and Reviews" and "Under the Microscope" in *Swinburne Replies*, ed. Clyde K. Hyder (Syracuse, 1966).

100. Gifford . . . 'found.' Cf. Gifford's note on the song "Oh do not wanton with those eyes," *Works*, VIII, 307.

100. Frank (Francis) Davison (c. 1575–c. 1619), editor of the last Elizabethan lyric anthology, *Poetical Rhapsody* (1602), is particularly noted for his short madrigals.

101. 'the admirable Epode' . . . *Love's Martyr*. Printed as the eleventh poem in *The Forest*. Cf. Gifford's note on *The Praeludium, Works*, VIII, 260–261.

102. "μόγον . . . ἀποστατεῖ": "From Death alone, of all the divinities, the goddess Persuasion stands aloof" (Fragment 161.4).

103. 'that women . . . shadows.' This song is printed in *The Forest* as the seventh poem.

103. address 'to Heaven.' The "opening couplet" of "To Heaven," the last poem printed in *The Forest*, is "Good and great GOD, can I not thinke of thee,/ But it must, straight, by melancholy be?" Cf. Gifford's note on the poem, *Works*, VIII, 280.

103. the second of the three. A short poem entitled "An Hymn to God the Father."

104. 'We will . . . Pro-me-the-an.' *Prometheus Unbound,* IV.156–158.

104. 'And from . . . her face.' From the fourth poem in the series, "Her Triumph," ll. 17–18.

104. Gifford . . . 'praise.' Cf. Gifford's note on the ninth poem in the series, "Her Man Described by her Own Dictamen," *Works*, VIII, 304.

105. "I wish . . . mine." "Against Jealousie," ll. 7–8, in *The Underwood*, X.

106. The four . . . Jonson. *The Underwood*, XXXVIII–XLI; the second (XXXIX) is now recognized to have been written by Donne.

107. "So may . . . sleep." "An Epistle to a friend," ll. 14–15, *The Underwood*, XXXVII; actually the two lines quoted are part of a triplet.

108. Coleridge . . . '*The Fox.*' *Table Talk* (August 20, 1833) in *Miscellaneous Criticism*, ed. Raysor, p. 427.

108–109. he proclaimed . . . King James II. "To my L. the King, On the Christning His second Sonne IAMES," *The Underwood*, LXXXII.

109. Gifford . . . 'Pindar.' The poem is "To the immortall memorie, and friendship of that noble paire, Sir LVCIVS CARY, and Sir H. Morison," *The Underwood*, LXX. For Gifford's comment, see *Works*, IX, 8.

110. elegy on the Marchioness of Winchester. *The Underwood*, LXXXIII.

110. elegiac . . . Venetia Stanley. *The Underwood,* LXXXIV.

110–111. *intus et in cute:* "within and on the surface" (Persius, *Satires,* III.30).

111. If the report . . . translation. Cf. *Conversations with Drummond,* 1. 694. It is difficult to determine by the syntax of the remark whether the opinion is Jonson's or Drummond's.

111–112. "Si torrere" . . . "toast." The apparent ridiculousness of Jonson's colloquial translation of the line from Horace, *Odes,* IV.i, in "To Venus," 1. 12, *The Underwood,* LXXXVI, is largely the result of semantic change and Renaissance physiological theory. In Jonson's day the liver was believed to be the seat of sexual passion. A modern (and unpoetic) rendering of the line would be "If you are seeking an appropriate heart to inflame."

112. Fate . . . prose works. The commentary is described in *Conversations with Drummond,* ll. 82–85 and 416–417; and its destruction by fire in 1623 is indicated in "An Execration upon Vulcan," ll. 89–90, *The Underwood,* XLIII.

113. Abraham Fraunce (fl. 1587–1633), associated with the Countess of Pembroke's circle, was the author of *Amintas Dale* (1592), noted for its metrical audacity. Jonson is reported to have said that Fraunce "in his English Hexameters was a Foole" (*Conversations with Drummond,* ll. 53–54).

113. Gabriel Harvey (1545?–1630), an undistinguished poet, was a leader in the attempt to impose classical quantitative prosody on English poetry. Juniper's misuse of words in *The Case is Altered* may in part

be patterned on Harvey, considered to be a pedant by his contemporaries.

113. 'The bellman' . . . away. Sir Walter Scott, *Rob Roy*, Chap. II. Swinburne has misquoted by substituting "verses" for "lines" in Scott's novel.

113. Gifford . . . 'meaning." *Works*, IX, 127.

114. "Meanwhile . . . hail." V.ii.56–57. Cf. C. Day Lewis' poetic translation, "At this stage a murmur, a growling began to be heard/ In the sky: soon followed a deluge of rain and hail together" (Aeneid, IV.160–161 [Garden City, New York, 1952]).

114. *Proh* . . . *fidem*: "By the good faith of the gods and men!" A variation of the interjection appears in Terence, *Hecyra*, II.i.1.

115. Théophile Gautier (1811–1872), French poet, critic, and novelist, was a leading exponent of the "art for art's sake" school of criticism. He is particularly known for his criticism on art and drama.

115. Browne, William (1591–1643?), is praised by Jonson in a poem prefixed to the second book of Browne's *Pastorals* published in 1616. The poem is reprinted in Herford and Simpson, VIII, 386.

115. Brome, Richard (c. 1590–c. 1652), was perhaps the closest follower of the "Sons of Ben." The bond is described as a master-servant relationship that has ripened into friendship by Jonson in his commendatory verse for Brome's *The Northern Lass* (1632). See Herford and Simpson, VIII, 409–410.

115. May, Thomas (1595–1650), was praised by Jonson for his translation of Lucan's *Pharsalia*, published in 1627 (Herford and Simpson, VIII, 395).

115. Stephens, John (fl. 1615), was commended by

Jonson for his play, *Cynthia's Revenge*, when it was published in 1613 (Herford and Simpson, VIII, 383).

115. Rutter, Joseph (fl. 1633–1640), was apparently a member of the Tribe of Ben. His first play, *The Shepherd's Holiday*, was published in 1635, and Jonson contributed commendatory verses (Herford and Simpson, VIII, 414–415).

115. Wright, Thomas (fl. 1604), authored *The Passions of the Mind in General*, to which Jonson paid tribute in one of his rare sonnets when the work was published in 1604 (Herford and Simpson, VIII, 370).

115. Warre, James, is known only for his *Touchstone of Truth* (1621), "a Puritan compendium of Scripture references on points of conduct as well as controversy." The authorship of the commendatory verses attributed to Jonson in the second edition (1624) is questionable (Herford and Simpson, XI, 146).

115. Filmer, Edward (d. 1669), published *French Court Airs* (1629), translations of French songs by Pierre Guedron and Antoine Boesset, which Jonson commended in verse (Herford and Simpson, VIII, 401–402).

116. Mr. Burges, John, was a clerk of the Exchequer to whom Jonson addressed two poems (*The Underwood*, LV and LVII).

116. Mr. Squib, Arthur, a teller of the Exchequer, was the recipient of two verse epistles written by Jonson (*The Underwood*, XLV and LIV).

117. Landor's principle . . . orthography. Cf. "Samuel Johnson and John Horne (Tooke)" and "Archdeacon Hare and Landor" in *Imaginary Conversations*. For a critique of Landor's theory, see Thomas De Quincey, "Orthographic Mutineers; With a Special Reference to

the Works of Walter Savage Landor," *Tait's Magazine* (March, 1847).

117. "Alii . . . inest": "Some not without reason write these words *abil, stabil, fabul* to resemble their sources *habilis, stabilis, fabula*, which is truer; but it serves no practical purpose. For when one listens more closely, the sound is neither that of an *i* or a *u*, but an indeterminate sound, having the nature of a vowel, which naturally exists in these liquid consonants" (Chap. IV, ll. 99–112 notes). The words *haud consulto* ("not without reason") in the first line of the quotation were added in the third folio and are not considered authoritative by Herford and Simpson (VIII, 489). The source of the quotation is Sir Thomas Smith's *De recta & emendata Linguae Anglicae scriptione* (Paris, 1568), though Jonson inserts the etymological notion (*a fontibus . . . verius*). See Herford and Simpson, XI, 180–181.

117. Jonson's view . . . 'writing.' *The English Grammar*, Chap. IV, ll. 241–255.

121. anonymous interlude . . . 'godfather.' *Works*, IX, 327. The entertainment was written to celebrate the christening of Charles Cavendish (born May 20, 1620), the second son of the Earl of Devonshire (Herford and Simpson, VII, 767).

121. "Macte . . . labore": "Bravo! By your work both writers and readers." The sentence is concluded in the next line, "*Per te alij vigeant, per te alij videant*": "may through you be strengthened and may through you understand." An English translation of the lines to be literal must be inexact and redundant. The poem was contributed to Thomas Farnaby's *Iunii Iuuenalis et Auli Persii Flacci Satyrae* (1612), and is reprinted in Herford and Simpson, VIII, 381. Herford and Simpson reject

Swinburne's argument that the verse was not by Jonson (XI, 135).

122. 'Les chassepots partiraient d'eux-mêmes': "The rifles would go off by themselves."

122. 'a fragment . . . *Eupheme*.' Gifford, *Works*, IX, 341.

122. text . . . *Annalia Dubrensia*. "An Epigram to my Iovial, Good Freind *Mr. Robert Dover*, on his Great Instauration of his Hunting, and Dauncing at *Cotswold*" (Herford and Simpson, VIII, 415–416).

123. *double . . . drop*. Herford and Simpson reject Swinburne's conjecture (VIII, 415).

123. Gifford's explanation . . . *vie. Works*, I, 101.

123. error . . . 'Light.' "Epitaph on Katherine, Lady Ogle." Herford and Simpson print "in the sight/ Of Angells" (VIII, 400). Gifford is in error.

123. additional scenes to *The Spanish Tragedy*. See note to p. 58 above.

124. allegoric ode. Prefixed to Hugh Holland's *Pancharis* (1603). This poem is reprinted in Herford and Simpson, VIII, 365–369.

124. Pindaric ode . . . Sir Henry Morison. See note to p. 109 above.

125. 'on this side idolatry.' From Jonson's comment on Shakespeare: "I lov'd the man, and doe honour his memory (on this side Idolatry) as much as any" (*Discoveries*, ll. 654–655).

129. Jonson's notes . . . superior to Bacon's. The comparison that follows may have been prompted in part by Cunningham's comment that Jonson "was filled with the very spirit" of Bacon in *Discoveries (Works*, IX, 494).

130. essay . . . 'dissimulation.' Bacon's *Essayes or Counsels, Civill and Morall* (1625), No. VI.

130. 'of all . . . honest.' Swinburne is paraphrasing Drummond: "of all stiles he loved most to be named honest" (*Conversations with Drummond*, 1. 631).

131. fourth scene . . . *Count Julian.* I.iv.31–49.

133. *"Non . . . fuere"*: "They have not been our masters but our leaders." The quoted passage derives from Vives, *In Libros de Disciplinis Praefatio* (*Opera*, I, 324–325). See Herford and Simpson, XI, 217–218.

133. *"Patet . . . relictum est"*: "Truth lies open to all: it has not yet been preempted. Much of it remains for future generations." Herford and Simpson accept Swinburne's emendation of *relictum* (VIII, 567).

134. *'opere pascitur'*: "it is fed by labor." The quoted passage is basically a translation from Vives, *De Causis Corruptarum Artium* (*Opera*, 1555, I, 326). See Herford and Simpson, XI, 218.

134–135. 'Æqua . . . improbari': "There is equal praise in being praised by the praise-worthy, and being condemned by the base."

135. The following . . . "knows none." Swinburne is apparently applying the quotation to Charles Parnell (1846–1891), the leader of the Irish cause for legislative independence, against which Swinburne wrote poems in 1886, 1887, and 1889. See Georges Lafourcade, *Swinburne: A Literary Biography* (New York, 1932), pp. 285–289, for a discussion of Swinburne's political attitude toward the Irish Question. The "present political application" of the quotation appears to refer to the Parnell "case" in Parliament. After the *Times* published letters implicating Parnell in a conspiracy to attain absolute independence for Ireland and other crimes, a

commission was established in 1888 to investigate the charges; but on February 21, 1889, after this part of the book had appeared in print in *The Fortnightly Review*, Richard Piggott confessed that the letters were forgeries, and Parnell was exonerated.

136. 'courtesy' . . . 'country.' Herford and Simpson have adopted Swinburne's suggested emendation (VIII, 577).

139. admiration . . . our time. The reference is to Browning, whose admiration of Euripides is demonstrated in *Belaustion's Adventures*, which includes a transcript of Euripides' *Alcestis* and *Aristophanes' Apology*, a vindication of Euripides.

139. "That the . . . Euripides." The source of this couplet has not been found; it is possible that Swinburne composed it for the occasion, for he used the same final rhyme, "insipid ease/ . . . Euripides," in a parody of Elizabeth Barrett Browning. The syntax that immediately precedes the quotation and that of the quotation itself is ambiguous: Swinburne may be referring to a contemporary as "the huckster of pathos," but positive identification has not been possible.

142. 'he esteemed . . . perish.' *Conversations with Drummond*, ll. 117–118 and l. 196.

143. Mérimée, Prosper (1803–1870), French novelist and historian, was particularly noted for perpetrating literary hoaxes.

143. revolt of the Tartars. Cf. De Quincey's tale entitled *Revolt of the Tartars*.

143. Clara Gazul's . . . *La Guzla*. Successful hoaxes perpetrated by Mérimée. *Le Théâtre de Clara Gazul* (1825) purported to be translations of six plays by a

Spanish actress called Clara Gazul, and the Illyrian ballads of *La Guzla* (1827) purported to be translations of Illyrian national songs and poems; both works were written by Mérimée.

145. insulting reference . . . judgment. In the lines that follow in Jonson's note, Marlowe is slighted in the reference to "the *Tamerlanes*, and *Tamber-Chams* of the Late Age, which had nothing in them, but the *scenicall* strutting, and furious vociferation, to warrant them to the ignorant gapers" (ll. 777–779). Jonson refers to Marlowe's "mighty line" in "To the Memory of . . . Mr. William Shakespeare . . . ," l. 30, prefixed to the First Folio (1623) of Shakespeare's works.

147. 'the boon Delphic god,' . . . Apollo. Cf. Shakerley Marmion's poem "On the Apollo" reprinted in Herford and Simpson, XI, 361.

148. The note . . . speaker. *Discoveries*, ll. 862–898. Jonson's entire discussion is taken from M. Seneca, *Controversiae*, III, praefatio 1–7, and I, praefatio 6; the analysis (ll. 886–898) is of Cassius Severus, though it apparently is applied to Bacon by Jonson. See Herford and Simpson, XI, 241.

148. magnificent tribute . . . adversity. *Discoveries*, ll. 915–923.

148. royalist as Fletcher. Cf. Coleridge's comment on Beaumont and Fletcher as "the most servile *jure divino* royalists," *Miscellaneous Criticism*, ed. Raysor, p. 69.

155. Amintor. Central victim of the king's lust in *The Maid's Tragedy*. Amintor remains a dedicated believer in the divinity of the king, even though it destroys him.

155. Aëcius. The emporer Valentinian's loyal general in *Valentinian* who takes his own life when unjustly

sentenced by the emperor rather than attempting to escape.

155. Archas. "The loyal subject" whose fidelity to the Duke of Muscovia is sorely tested but remains firm in *The Loyal Subject*.

155. Aubrey. Cousin to the Dukes of Normandy, Rollo and Otto, and a loyal subject in the face of tyranny in *The Bloody Brother, or Rollo, Duke of Normandy*.

156. La Rochefoucauld, François de (1613–1680), moralist and author of *Réflexions ou sentences et maximes morales* (better known as *Maximes*) and *Reflexions diverses*.

156. Chamfort, Nicholas-Sébastien Roch (1741–1794), dramatist and critic, but most famous as the author of *Maximes, caractères et anecdotes*.

158–159. case of Somerset and Overbury. Sir Thomas Overbury, who had been a friend of the Earl of Somerset and had cautioned Somerset against marrying the Countess of Essex, the former Lady Frances Howard, was imprisoned and subsequently poisoned. See note to p. 46 above.

160 n.1. Swinburne's emendation is adopted by Herford and Simpson, VIII, 606.

162. rival poets . . . court. In the reign of Charles II it was common for the poets to curry favor with those at the center of power. Dryden, for instance, gained the patronage of Lady Castlemain, Charles' first royal mistress, and celebrated her beauty and greatness of soul in his fourth verse epistle (*The Works of John Dryden*, revised and corrected by George Saintsburg, XI [Edinburgh, 1885], 18–21).

162. 'he would . . . thunder.' *Coriolanus,* III.i.255–257.

163. Epictetus (c. 60–?), Phrygian Stoic philosopher, whose teachings were recorded by his disciple Arrian in the *Discourses* and *Encheiridion.*

163. Aurelius, Marcus (121–180), Roman emperor and author of *Meditations,* which expresses an eclectic philosophy with a Stoic basis.

165. 'Louer tout . . . dénigrer tout': "To praise everything is another way of disparaging everything."

166. 'not of . . . all time.' See note to p. 70 above.

166. paid such . . . old master. Jonson paid tribute to his schoolmaster, William Camden (1551–1623), in Epigram XIV, where he addresses Camden as "most reverend head," and in dedications of the 1601 quarto edition of *Cynthia's Revels* and of the 1616 folio edition of *Every Man in his Humour.*

166. illustrious . . . principle. *Boswell's Life of Johnson,* ed. G. B. Hill, rev. L. F. Powell (Oxford, 1934), I, 46 and II, 406.

166. Charles Kingsley . . . 'punishments.' Contrary to Swinburne's implication that Kingsley favored flogging, Kingsley's wife reports: "Punishment was a thing little known in his house. Corporal punishment was never allowed. His own childish experience of the sense of degradation and unhealthy fear it produced, of the antagonism it called out between a child and its parents, a pupil and his teachers gave him a horror of it" (*Letters and Memories of Charles Kingsley,* ed. by his wife [New York and London, 1899], II, 38).

166. denounced . . . by Quintilian. *Institutio Oratoria,* I.iii.

168. Bentley, Richard (1662–1742), was a brilliant textual critic highly regarded for his emendations in classical texts; he established more scientific methods for textual criticism than had earlier prevailed.

168. Porson, Richard (1759–1808), was a classical scholar particularly known for his textual criticism on Greek drama and Homer.

170. Of Spenser . . . Landor. Landor's dislike of Spenser's poetic allegory was well-known, but he did find "the 'Faery Queen' the most delightful book in the world to fall asleep upon by the seaside," as he expressed in a letter to a friend (Richard Hengist Horne, *A New Spirit of the Age* [London, 1844], I, 174–175).

170. 'Spenser's . . . matter.' *Conversations with Drummond*, 1. 20.

171. verdict . . . Hugo. Explicit preference of Plautus over Terence has not been found in the works of either Swift or Hugo.

175. Johnson . . . 'understanding.' *Boswell's Life of Johnson*, ed. Hill, rev. Powell, IV, 313. Swinburne paraphrases; Boswell records Johnson to have said, "Sir, I have found you an argument; but I am not obliged to find you an understanding."

177. The remarks . . . 'style.' *Discoveries*, ll. 2161–2289. This discussion is taken from John Hoskyns' *Directions for Speech and Style*. See Herford and Simpson XI, 276–278.

177. "oftentimes [lost] by affectation." The error that Swinburne finds is the result of Jonson having omitted a line from Hoskyns in the transcription. See Herford and Simpson, VIII, 631.

179. lack . . . *Othello*. See note to p. 25 above.

181. if Ben Jonson . . . Dr. Athanasius Dogberry.
Alfred Waites delivered an address before the New York
Shakespeare Society on January 24, 1889, arguing that
Jonson wrote the *Essays* and other Baconian works. His
argument was published as "Did Ben Jonson Write
Bacon's Works?" in *Shakespeariana*, VI (1889), 145–157
(April), 241–259 (June), and 298–313 (July), but since
this part of Swinburne's book was first published in
October 1888, Swinburne must have learned of Waites'
theory before it was published.